Resource and Environmental Sciences Series

General Editors:
Sir Alan Cottrell, FRS
Professor T.R.E. Southwood, FRS

Food, Energy and Society

David Pimentel and Marcia Pimentel

College of Agriculture and Life Sciences and Division of Nutritional Sciences, Cornell University, Ithaca, New York

Edward Arnold

© D. and M. Pimentel 1979

First published 1979 by
Edward Arnold (Publishers) Ltd
41 Bedford Square, London WCIB 3DQ
Reprinted 1982

British Library Cataloguing in Publication Data

Pimentel, David
   Food, energy and society. – (Resource and
   environmental sciences series).
   1. Agriculture – Energy consumption
   2. Food industry and trade – Energy consumption
   I. Title   II. Pimentel, Marcia   III. Series
   338.1'9   S494.5. E5

ISBN 0 7131 2761 9

Photo typeset in India by
The Macmillan Co. of India Ltd.
Bangalore–560001

Printed in Great Britain by
Whitstable Litho Ltd., Whitstable, Kent

Preface

Over the centuries man has used energy from many sources to grow food, provide shelter, protect health and improve his lifestyle. Both the energy source, be it the sun or atomic fission, and its relative abundance have influenced man's activities. As societal groupings have changed so has energy use. Thus, the early savage who hunted and gathered his food in the wild depended primarily on his own energies. Today much of the world's population is able to rely on fossil fuels, while many in the developing countries must be content to use animal power, manpower, and fuel wood.

Regardless of the type of energy used, man always has had to expend it to meet his basic need for food. Ample fossil energy supplies have enabled man to keep up with the ever-increasing human birth rate. Birth rates remain high while energy reserves, especially fossil fuel supplies, are diminishing. So now, as we look forward to the year 2000 when the world population to be fed will have nearly doubled over present levels, we wonder what strategies can be developed to meet such a tremendously increased demand.

Before plans can be made much information needs to be gathered about the energy costs of the diverse food production systems now employed. These costs must be balanced against the supplies of energy that will be available.

Thus, the aim of this book is to explore the interdependencies of food, energy, and their impacts on society. These analyses we hope will be a basis for planning and implementing policies of individuals and nations as they face the inevitable dilemma – how can everyone be fed, given the limited resources of the earth.

This book represents the cooperative efforts of many people. With sincere appreciation we wish to acknowledge the assistance of our graduate students for help in collecting data; the editorial assistance of Ms. Nancy Goodman, Ms. Beth French, and Mr. George McClellan; and the manuscript typing of Ms. Deborah Alesbury and Ms. Beth French.

Ithaca, New York   D. Pimentel
1979   M. Pimentel

Contents

1 Energy and Society

Introduction

Basic to man's survival are adequate food, water and shelter; maintenance of health and personal security are equally important. Closely interrelated with these life-essentials is an adequate energy supply, for energy in some form or other is used in attaining food, water, shelter, security, and protecting man from parasites and predators.

Over the centuries man has used energy from many sources. Starting with his own energy and sunlight, he then progressed to wood fuel, draft-animal power, and water and wind power. Later, engine power was developed, fueled by wood, coal, petroleum and nuclear energy. Man has used energy to modify or manipulate land, water, plants and animals to provide himself with food, clothing and supplies to provide shelters. Finding, controlling and using energy has enabled man to progress from a primitive life to a settled civilized state. Man alone of all animals can think creatively and utilize science and technology, and has been able to use energy and other environmental resources to his own advantage.

Energy is also expended to control disease organisms; to obtain, purify and store water; to produce pesticides for the control of disease vectors; to produce antibiotics and other chemical drugs; and to implement diverse public health measures.

While public health is one aspect of security, both security and stability are also associated with the protection of one man from another, or one group of people and their resources from encroachment by rival groups. Social harmony depends not only on the rules established by governments but also on the effectiveness of the police and military forces used to enforce the laws. Governments, police and military forces all require the expenditure of enormous amounts of energy. In the so-called 'civilized society' of the developed nations of the world today, significantly more energy is used by the government, police and military than is used to produce food for the population being governed.

The availability of surplus energy enabled man to develop a societal structure more complex than that of the early hunter-gatherers. The present state of energy use represents a dramatic change from that of the distant past when finding adequate food was man's prime concern and dominated his activities. White (1943) proposed that the evolution of man occurred in the following three major stages: (1) 'savagery' – people were hunter-gatherers living on wild food; (2) 'barbarianism' – early agricultural and pastoral societies; and (3) 'civilization' – development of engines and intensive use of fossil energy to produce food and other necessities.

These steps are all related to changes in energy supplies used by man. In fact, White (1943) felt that man would have 'remained on the level of savagery indefinitely if he had not learned to augment the amount of energy under his control'. This includes the total quantity of energy controlled by man and the surplus energy available to him above that needed for his essentials of food, clothing, shelter and public health.

Development of Societies and Energy

Hunter-gathering societies were small, rarely over 500 individuals (Service, 1962; Lee and DeVore, 1976) and simple (Bews, 1973). Because securing food and shelter consumed so much time and energy, other individual and collective activities scarcely existed. With the development of agriculture, however, more food, fibre resources and surplus energy became available. Concurrently, a greater interdependence among people and a greater incentive for increased productivity evolved in human societies. An equally important factor was that as the quantities of food produced increased, the stability of food supplies also increased. Societies that had once been seminomadic, following their food supply, gained in security and permanence.

Even in early agricultural societies food production still dominated man's activities and, as a result, his social interaction remained relatively narrow. The introduction of draft-animal power to agricultural production freed more of man's time and energy. This surplus energy and increased free time enabled him to participate in various activities and, as a result, social systems became more complex.

The water wheel and windmill added new sources of energy that man used primarily in his food system. Now, instead of using draft animals that required energy for feed and care, man used water and wind power. With this change, man had more power at his disposal and at a lower cost (calculated as man's energy input) than in the past. In this way the amount of surplus energy available to society was greatly increased.

Water and wind, as added resources of power and the subsequent reduction of dependence on animal power, fostered the development of trading and transport between groups of people. Under conditions

of improved communication the exchange of resources and
ideas increased between groups. Technical advances spread more
easily than ever before. Further development of science and
technology resulted in the building and use of sailing ships, which
enhanced communication, transportation and trade between larger
groups. With these changes came greater diversity in man's activities
and specialities of farming, sailing, trading and industry developed.

The invention of the steam engine was a highly significant mile-
stone in energy use for it signalled the beginning of the use of fossil
fuels as energy sources. This, and later engines that used coal and
oil as fuels, gave man immense power to control his environment
and to change the total economic, political and social structure of
society. Along with these changes came greater stability and even
greater specialization of work.

Energy from Fire

Although primitive man feared fire, he learned to control and use it
about a half million years ago. Fire helped ward off large animal
predators and helped clear vegetation, which provided further
protection against predators and other enemies. Campfires provided
needed warmth when climate was cold.

In addition, fires made possible the cooking of meats, vegetables
and fruits. Indeed, cooking made many foods easier to eat and
better tasting. Some foods, such as cereals, were more easily
digested after cooking. Perhaps more important was the fact that
heating reduced the danger of illness from parasitic and disease
organisms that often contaminate the raw foods. For instance, heat
kills several parasitic worms (e.g. *Trichinella*) that are commonly
found in raw meat from various animals and will cause severe, even
fatal, illness in man.

Cooking also destroyed microorganisms often responsible for
food spoilage. In this way, cooking foods reduced man's exposure to
many debilitating parasitic and disease organisms, improved the
flavour and digestibility of foods, and reduced the chances of spoilage. Also important was the use of fire to dry surplus meats and
plant foods, and thereby preserve them for long periods of time.
This simple method of preservation thus stabilized and enhanced the
availability of food supplies long after the time of harvest.

When primitive agriculture was becoming established (about
10 000 years ago), fire was used to help clear trees and shrubs from
the crop land; this simple procedure also helped eliminate weeds
that competed with the crops. The incorporation of burned trees
and shrubs into soil added nutrients to the soil and made the land
more productive for crop culture. Fire was also employed to main-

tain grazing land for wild animals as with buffalo in America.

The principal source of fuel for fires was wood from trees and shrubs, although some grasses and other vegetation were also burned. With a relatively small population of humans on earth ample supplies of renewable energy in the form of wood were available. Coal was known in some regions, but this fuel source did not find widespread use during man's early history.

Energy and the Structure of Societies

The societies of early hunter-gatherers had minimal structure. At most, a chief or group of elders led the camp or village. Most of these leaders had to hunt and gather along with other members because the surpluses of food and other vital resources were seldom enough to support a full-time chief or village council.

The development of agriculture changed this monotypic work pattern. The early agricultural family could reap 3–10 kg of grain from each kilogram of seed planted. Part of this food/energy surplus was returned to the community, and provided support for non-farmers such as chieftains or village councils, medicine men, priests and even warriors. The non-farmers of these early societies improved leadership, stability and security for the farming population, thus enabling it to increase surplus food/energy yields.

Under conditions favourable for agriculture, and with improved agricultural technology, consistent surpluses were produced and, as a result, larger population groups or towns developed. With the concentration of populations in larger towns and cities, further specialization of tasks evolved. Specialists such as masons, carpenters, blacksmiths, merchants, traders and sailors were more efficient in their use of time and energy than unskilled people. The goods and services provided by artisan-technologists brought about an improved quality of life, a higher standard of living and, for most societies, increased stability.

Egypt during the reign of the Pharoahs is an outstanding example of an early society that possessed environmental resources favourable for the establishment of a stable agriculture but also developed effective agricultural technology (Cottrell, 1955). The Nile carried water and valuable nutrients to the farmlands, replacing the soil nutrients removed by harvested grain and other foods. By its yearly flooding the Nile deposited nutrient-rich silt on the farmland and kept the land productive. It was also a reliable source of water for irrigation. Additionally, and as important, was the warm Egyptian climate that was highly favourable for crop production. This productive agricultural system supported the 95 % of the Egyptian population that was directly involved in agriculture (Fig. 1.1), and

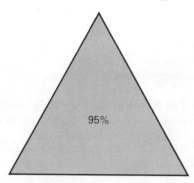

Fig. 1.1 During the age of the Pharoahs and pyramid projects Egypt had a population of 3 million. About 95 % of society was involved in agriculture. The surplus energy of about 5 % was utilized for the Pharoahs and the construction of the great pyramids.

provided enough surplus food to sustain the 5 % of the population who did no work in agriculture (Cottrell, 1955).

Relatively little food energy was necessary to support the small ruling class. Egypt's naturally isolated location provided protection from invasion without the necessity of large energy expenditure to maintain a military class. As a result, the 5 % of the population not involved in agriculture could be and were used by the Pharoahs as slave-labour to build pyramids and stock them with goods and materials for a life Egyptians believed would come after life on earth.

During this period the Egyptian population remained relatively constant because of the demands made by the rulers on the population for slaves. As soon as surplus men were sufficiently mature for work they were assigned to pyramid construction. These men were forced to put in long hours of hard work and were literally 'worked to death' during a few years of slave labour. When they died they were replaced with new surplus labour. All this was done without jeopardizing the fundamental agricultural system that involved the efforts of almost all the Egyptian people.

During the age of the Pharoahs, which spanned the years from 2780 to 1625 B.C. (Fakhry, 1969), Egypt had a population of about 3 million, much less than the 38 million of today. A 5 % food/energy surplus from about 3 million people is not much. On a per capita basis this ranges from 100 to 150 kcal per day (Cottrell, 1955) or an equivalent of 10–15 kg of wheat per person per year. Based on 3 million people, this totals about $30–45 \times 10^6$ kg of wheat surplus per year.

The construction of the Cheops pyramid over a 20-year span used an amount of energy that equalled the surplus energy produced in the lifetime of about 3 million Egyptian people (Cottrell, 1955). During the construction period the pyramid work force was about 100 000 slaves per year. Assuming each slave was provided with 300–400 kg of food per year, the total cost would be $30–45 \times 10^6$ kg food or the entire surplus food/energy from the Egyptian agricultural society.

In later periods in the history of Egypt, similar levels of surpluses were used to support large military forces that conquered some of Egypt's neighbours. These military operations secured some additional land and food and often the conquered people were brought back to Egypt as slaves. But the long distances over desert areas that the Egyptian forces had to travel and transport supplies naturally limited the military operations. Large quantities of energy had to be expended simply to protect the supply routes and transport military supplies.

At other times, when the population increased to large numbers relative to the land and agricultural resources, surpluses of agricultural resources were not available in Egypt. Under these relatively over-populated conditions and with shortages instead of surpluses, the Egyptian society was just able to maintain itself. Sometimes, under these stress conditions, civil strife and social problems developed. These conditions often led to a decline in population numbers because these unstable societies were not productive in agriculture or any other essential activity.

Thus, Egypt's early history is an excellent example of the role that energy, as measured by food surpluses, played in the structure and activities of an early society. Although the structures of today's societies are far more complex, energy continues to be an important factor.

Food as a Focal Point of Societies

One of the most basic and essential needs of man and nature as a whole is an adequate supply of food. In natural communities, the entire structure and function of the population that makes up the community revolves about food as an energy source (Elton, 1927). In more primitive societies food was also used as an exchange item long before money was used. Man exchanged surpluses of crops and in this way not only improved his own diet but interacted with other groups.

The evolution of species populations within communities appears to be influenced by the relation of food supplies to demand. As with human societies, stability has advantages for a biotic community's survival and therefore is an important evolutionary trend (Pimentel, 1961 and 1968). Evolved balance in supply-demand economies of species populations contributes to the relative stability that is observed in these dynamic community systems.

The major reason food and energy are considered to be critical resources for natural communities (including man's) is the limited amount of solar energy that is fixed or converted into plant biomass by growing plants. Plants fix less than 0.1% of the light energy reaching the earth. Before fossil fuels were used, both man and other animals shared that portion of the sun's energy captured by plants and subsequently changed to food/energy.

In prehistoric times, man acknowledged the importance of food in his life. This is revealed in the many pictures of animals and food plants that prehistoric people painted in the caves where they lived and on the implements they used (Fig. 1.2).

Fig. 1.2 Drawing of a cow and several small horses in the painted cave of Lascaux, France (Brodrick, 1949).

The high priority given to food by man is well documented throughout history. Not only does Egyptian art work picture various food crops and livestock, but grains and other food items were customarily buried with the dead. Another striking example is the Mayan civilization of Central America, which depended on corn (maize) as its staple food. The frequent appearance of corn in their numerous sculptures and paintings emphasizes the importance of corn to the Mayans.

Historically, there appears to be no other resource that man has valued more than food. This is evident not only in drawings, sculptures and other art work, but also in many of the religious and cultural ceremonies and festivities that celebrate successful harvests.

Use of Energy in Food Systems

One measure of the relative importance of food in society as a whole is the amount of energy and labour that is devoted to providing food for man. In prehistoric times, about 95 % of the total energy expended to maintain the family was used for food production. This included hunting and gathering, transporting the food back to camp and preparing the food for consumption.

Even today, in some developing countries agriculture dominates the economy to the extent that the energy expended by the population in its food system ranges from 60–80 % (RSAS, 1975). This contrasts with many developed countries, where the proportion of energy devoted to food production ranges only from 15–35 %. For example, in the United States and United Kingdom, the amount of energy expended in food production represents about 16 % of the total energy used (FEA, 1975; Leach, 1976). As in the developing countries, this energy expenditure includes production, processing, distribution and preparation of food in the total system.

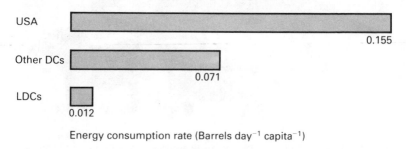

Energy consumption rate (Barrels day^{-1} capita^{-1})

Fig. 1.3 Energy consumption rates in the United States, other developed countries (DCs), and less developed countries (LDCs) (Penner and Icerman, 1974).

Although in the United States the proportion of energy used in the food system is only 16.5 %, the total quantity of energy used is several times that used in the less complex societies of the developing countries (Fig. 1.3). Specifically, in the United States three times as much energy is expended per capita for food than is expended per capita in developing countries for all energy-consuming activities including food production. This comparison emphasizes once again the energy-intensive life-style that has developed in such countries as the United States, especially since the ready availability of fossil-fuel energy supplies.

2 Energy and Manpower

Energy and Work

Energy is the capacity to do work. Although energy is found in
many forms (Table 2.1), all forms have the capacity to do work.
Light energy, coming from the sun, is the most important form for
maintenance of all life on earth. Plants have the capacity to capture
or 'fix' light energy and convert it into chemical energy for use by
the plants themselves and the animals that eat them. Although solar
energy is used in many of man's activities, it functions most promi-
nently in agricultural and forestry production.

Electrical energy is used for radio, radar, microwaves and TV
waves. The lifting or moving of objects by man or machine is a
form of mechanical energy. Another form of energy is heat that is
used for cooking and refrigeration. Magnetic energy, which results
from the interaction of positive and negative charged matter, can be
used to do work. Sound waves are also considered a form of energy.
A more recently discovered form of energy is nuclear energy, that is
released from the bound atomic particles in, for instance, uranium.
Since its discovery, man has found a way to use nuclear energy not
only for devastating bombs but also to produce electricity in
specially designed power plants.

Laws of Thermodynamics

The use or flow of energy is governed principally by the two laws of
thermodynamics. *The first law of thermodynamics states that energy
may be transformed from one type into another* (Table 2.1), *but can
never be created or destroyed.* For example, light energy can be
transformed into heat energy or into plant-food energy (chemical
energy). In the process of this transformation of light energy into
plant-food energy, no energy is lost or destroyed, only its form is
changed.

*The second law of thermodynamics states that no transformation of
energy will occur unless energy is degraded from a concentrated form
to a more dispersed form, and further that no transformation is 100%
efficient.*

The flow from a high energy source toward a lower energy source
is referred to as the stability principle. For example, if a hot object

Table 2.1 Some examples of energy conversion and energy converting devices (after Steinhart and Steinhart, 1974a).

To \ From	Mechanical	Thermal	Acoustical	Chemical	Electrical	Light
Mechanical	Oar Sail Jack Bicycle	Steam engine	Barograph Ear	Muscle contraction Bomb Jet engine	Electric motor Piezo-electric crystal	Photoelectric door opener
Thermal	Friction Brake Heat pump	Radiator	Sound absorber	Food Fuel	Resistor Spark plug	Solar cooker Greenhouse effect
Acoustical	Bell Violin Wind-up phonograph	Flame tube	Megaphone	Explosion	Telephone receiver Loudspeaker Thunder	
Chemical	Impact detonation of nitroglycerine	Endothermic chemical reactions		Growth and metabolism	Electrolysis	Photosynthesis Photochemical reactions
Electrical	Dynamo Piezo-electric crystal	Thermopile	Induction microphone	Battery Fuel cell	Transformer Magnetism	Solar cell
Light	Friction (sparks)	Thermoluminescence		Bioluminescence Candle	Light bulb Lightning	Fluorescence

is placed next to a cool object, heat will flow from the hot object to the cool, but never in reverse. Because the transformation is never 100 % efficient, the temperature of the cool object will rise, but not enough to account for all the energy that is transferred from the hot object. In this transfer some energy is dispersed into the environment. Consider the example of mixing a cup of boiling water with a cup of cold water. The temperature of the resulting mixture is slightly lower than would be calculated from the measured energy lost by the boiling water. The cold water is much warmer than it was initially, but because some of the heat energy is lost to the environment, it will not be as hot as expected from averaging the two initial temperatures.

The function of all biological systems, including crops, follows the second law of thermodynamics when solar energy (a high-energy form) is converted into chemical energy. Plants utilize this chemical energy in the process of building their own tissue. Some of the energy being changed from light to chemical energy is lost as heat that dissipates into the surrounding environment.

Measure of Energy

The basic units of energy measurement are the calorie, joule, Btu and watt. Heat is the one form of energy that does not have the direct ability to do work, but it does have the capacity to raise the temperature of matter or to change the state (solid, liquid, gas) of a colder substance. A calorie or gram-calorie is the amount of heat that is needed to raise 1 g of water 1°C at 15°C. The kilocalorie (kcal) or kilogram-calorie is 1000 gram-calories or the amount of heat needed to raise 1 kg of water 1°C at 15°C. In nutrition, the large Calorie that equals 1000 small calories or 1 kcal is used.

The British thermal unit (Btu) is the amount of heat needed to raise 1 1b of water 1°F and is equal to 252 calories or 0.252 kcal. One joule equals 0.24 calories (4186 J = 1 kcal) or 10^7 ergs. One joule is equal to 0.74 foot-pounds or 0.1 kg-metres. The watt is equal to 1 joule per second or 14.3 kcal per minute.

Work, measured in foot-pounds and requiring the expenditure or use of energy, is done at different rates. The term power is the time-rate at which work is done and/or energy is expended. Thus, the term joule/second means 1 joule energy was expended per second. The term *watt* is synonymous with 1 joule/second and is a concise way to express this much power.

Horsepower is another commonly used unit of power. One horsepower-hour (hp-h) is the capacity to do 33 000 foot-pounds of work per minute for one hour and is based on the ability of the average horse to lift 33 000 pounds one foot per minute for one hour. The maximum work capacity for a horse per day is about 10 hp-h, or a 10-hour work day.

One horsepower-hour or 33 000 foot-pounds of work per minute for one hour can be equated to heat energy. This amount of power will raise the temperature of 641 kg of water at 15°C by 1°C. Thus, when translated into kcal, one hp-h represents 641 kcal of heat energy.

One man working a 10-hour day produces the equivalent of only 1 hp-h. Thus, one manpower hour (mp-h) equals only about 1/10th of a horsepower hour; or one horse in one hour can accomplish the same amount of work as ten men in one hour. Horsepower and ox-power were some of the first substitutes for manpower and contributed to improving the quality of man's life. Certainly the people wielding hoes in early agriculture were more productive when they used oxen and horses.

The tremendous concentration of energy in a gallon (3.79 litres) of gasoline can be appreciated by comparing it to manpower. One gallon of gasoline contains about 31 000 kcal of potential energy. When this gallon of gasoline is used to operate a mechanical engine, which is about 20 % efficient in converting heat energy into mechanical energy, an equivalent of 6200 kcal of work can be achieved. This is equal to about 9.7 hp-h of work. Hence, from a single gallon of gasoline we can obtain the work equivalent of one horse working at capacity for nearly a 10-hour day. Further, one gallon of gasoline produces work equivalent to 97 manpower hours, or one man working eight hours a day, five days a week for about 2.5 weeks.

Biological Solar Energy Conversion in Agriculture

The survival of man and his ecosystem depends upon the efficiency of green plants as energy converters. They convert sunlight into food energy for themselves, man and other organisms. The total foundation of the life system, including agriculture, rests on this unique capacity of plants to change the radiated solar energy into stored chemical energy that is biologically useful material for man and other animals.

The solar energy reaching a hectare each day in the temperate region ranges from $15–40 \times 10^6$ kcal. Over one year's time the total solar energy received per hectare ranges from 1.1 to 1.8×10^{10} kcal, with 1.4×10^{10} kcal as a reliable average. This is equivalent to the energy potential of nearly 452 000 gallons (1.7×10^6 litres) of gasoline per year per hectare. This sounds like a large quantity of energy, and indeed it is when considered as a unit. But each square millimetre per day receives only 0.0038 kcal – only enough to raise the temperature of 3.8 ml of water 1°C.

Green plants are able to capture only a small percentage of the sunlight reaching the earth. Annually, the total light energy fixed by green plants in ecosystems is estimated at about 400×10^{15} kcal, divided equally between terrestrial and ocean ecosystems (Pimentel *et al.*, 1978). The amount of energy fixed by the world's plants amounts to less than 0.1 % of the total sunlight energy reaching the earth (Whittaker and Likens, 1975). Note that although the terrestrial systems cover only about a third of the earth, the plants in these systems fix about half of the total light energy captured.

When only the temperate zone is considered, we estimate only 0.07 % of the 1.4×10^{10} kcal sunlight (Reifsnyder and Lull, 1965) is fixed in these terrestrial ecosystems. Thus, the net energy fixed by plants in the temperate zone averages about 10×10^6 kcal ha^{-1} per year. Expressed as the dry weight of plant material, this amounts to an average yield of 2400 kg ha^{-1} per year, ranging from near zero in some rock and desert areas to 10 000 kg ha^{-1} in some swamps and marshes (Whittaker and Likens, 1975).

 In agricultural ecosystems, an estimated 15 × 10⁶ kcal of light energy (net production) is fixed per hectare per crop season. Even so this amounts to only about 0.1 % of the total solar energy reaching a hectare during the year and equals about 3500 kg ha^{-1} of dry biomass. The amount varies with the crop and ranges from 200 kg ha^{-1} for such crops as beans to 11 000 kg ha^{-1} for corn (maize) and sugar-cane (USDA, 1976a). By comparison, agricultural (crop) ecosystems produce an annual biomass per hectare that is slightly greater than the average of natural ecosystems. This is not surprising since crop plants are grown on the most productive soils and are often provided with ample moisture and added essential nutrients (fertilizers).

Under optimal conditions, during sunny days in midsummer and when the plants are nearing maturity, crops like corn and sugar-cane capture as much as 5 % of the light energy reaching the earth. Over the entire growing season in the temperate zone, however, the percentage of light energy captured by crops is less than 0.1 %. This represents the net energy that may be harvested in the form of plant material.

A significant quantity of captured energy is, of course, utilized by the plant itself. For example, a soybean plant uses about 25 % of the energy it collects for respiration and maintenance. About 5 % of the energy is diverted to provide food for the nitrogen-fixing bacteria that are symbionts with the soybean plant. Another 5–10 % is lost to pest populations that feed on the plant. The net yield in beans plus vegetation is about 65 % of the energy collected by the plant.

Most plants divert large proportions of the light energy they fix into their fruits and seeds. This ranges from 5 to 50 % of the total light energy fixed by the plant, and illustrates the high priority given by plants to reproduction (Harper, 1977).

Crop breeding techniques for the reallocation of energy in plants have been used to improve crop yields. For example, Grogan (personal communication, 1975) reported that one of the factors contributing to increased yields in the new breeds of corn has been changes in energy allocation within the plant. In particular, the size of tassel and quantity of pollen produced by the new corn breeds is reportedly less. The energy saved from the tassel and pollen production has been allocated to corn grain. With corn plants growing as densely as they do under normal cropping conditions, the smaller tassel and lesser amount of pollen is satisfactory for production of seed.

Renewable Biological Energy versus Fossil Fuel Energy

By the 16th century, England and France were running out of wood, their renewable energy resource (Nef, 1977). Wood was used to cook and prepare foods, and to heat the homes of the expanding population. It was also used to produce charcoal for the developing metal industry and to provide lumber for the growing ship-building and construction industries. Because of wood shortages, London and Paris were forced to turn to soft coal as a substitute (Cook, 1976). Since soft coal was a noxious fuel when burned, wood continued to be the preferred fuel, and those people who could pay the high price burned wood. At this time coal was used primarily for heating; its use as a source of energy to replace man and horse did not occur until about 200 years later.

Coal was used extensively, however, to fuel pumps in mining operations. As mines were dug deeper, water began seeping into the mines and caused serious flooding problems. The mine operators used windmills, hand pumps and windlasses to remove the water, but with poor results. Then, in 1698 Thomas Savery invented the first steam-powered pump to remove water from the mines. This pump, however, proved dangerous to operate and was never fully adopted. About 10 years later, Thomas Newcomen designed a new steam-powered pump that was much more effective than the Savery pump and was extensively employed in the mines. Thereafter coal could be mined more efficiently and a good supply was ready to replace the declining supply of fuel wood. (Note, it was not until nearly 100 years later that James Watt designed a truly efficient steam engine and pump. This effective pump, when it was finally operational, rapidly replaced the Newcomen steam pump.)

In the United States from 1700 to 1800, wood was the primary source of fuel. As late as 1850, more than 91 % of the energy used in the United States came from burning wood (EOP, 1977). During this period the United States had a much lower population density than Europe, and American forests had been harvested for only a relatively short period of time compared to European forests.

The supply of wood in the United States was sufficient in 1850 for two reasons. First, the population in the United States was about 1/10th the 217 million it is today. Second, the per capita use of energy in the United States was about 1/5th of today's use. Thus in 1850 the United States consumed only about 1/50th of the energy it consumes today. The conditions of a relatively small population and low per capita energy use made it possible for the forests and other vegetation to supply U.S. energy needs at that time. This is totally impossible today.

Even so, as early as 1850 the larger cities were having trouble maintaining adequate supplies of wood, because of the difficulty of transporting the wood from forest regions located far distant from the cities.

The Watt steam engine and the internal combustion engine developed in 1876, brought dramatic changes in energy consumption. These new fossil fuel-powered engines quickly replaced the less efficient wood powered engines, the horse and even manpower. Production of goods increased, expenditure of energy increased, and each decade has witnessed further use of the non-renewable fuel resources.

At present fossil fuel consumption is the highest it ever has been. Annual consumption for the world stands at about 62×10^{15} kcal and is increasing every year. The United States alone is consuming 29 % of this amount (18×10^{15} kcal) (FEA, 1976b). Fossil fuels account for 94 % of the total fuels consumed in the United States. Of this, petroleum represents 46 %, natural gas 30 %, and coal 18 % (FEA, 1976b). Hydroelectric energy accounts for 4 % and nuclear energy only 2 % of the total energy used.

The epoch of fossil fuel use, as viewed in perspective with the entire history of man, will truly be but a short interval (Fig. 2.1). Considering the more than one million years of man's existence on earth, the reliance on fossil fuels will be but a small 'blip' in history – 500–700 years or probably at most 0.001 % of the time man has been on earth. This is because fossil fuels are non-renewable natural resources and man has done little to conserve the earth's supply.

Oil and gas supplies will be the first fossil fuels to be depleted. Best estimates are that more than half of these fuels will be gone by the year 2000 (Hubbert, 1972). If oil alone were used to run all the

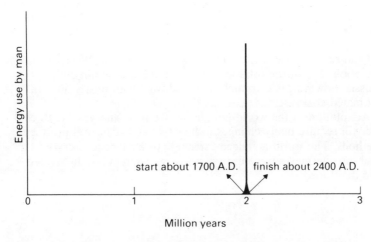

Fig. 2.1 The epoch of the use of fossil fuels in the history of man on earth.

power activities in the United States, U.S. oil reserves would last a mere 5 years (Hammond, 1972). Oil imports now amount to nearly 50 % of the oil consumed, and the question facing the United States is whether it can afford to pay the prices. In most of the Common Market countries of Europe the outlook is even bleaker, for about 98 % of the oil used is imported (SOEC, 1976). Such costly imports dangerously strain the economies of these nations and upset the balance of trade.

Coal reserves in the world are extensive and supplies should be ample for the next 100 years (Hubbert, 1972). There are, however, problems connected with greatly increased use of coal. A prime difficulty is the production of sulphur dioxide and other dangerous environmental pollutants when coal is burned. Further, at present we do not have the trained labour needed to increase greatly the coal mining efforts in many parts of the world.

Another problem in using coal is the method of mining. Strip mining, in particular, destroys land valued for food production and wildlife. On the average it is safer for miners, is more economical and requires less energy than deep mining. Strip mining is 80–90 % effective in recovering coal, compared with deep mining that is only 50 % effective. This is because in deep mining small coal seams cannot be economically mined, and some coal seams cannot be removed at all because of the danger of cave-ins.

The production of coal is less energy-costly than oil in both mining and transport costs. About 20 % of the potential energy is expended to mine and refine oil (Cervinka, 1978). The result is a yield of about 80 % at point of use. By comparison, coal has a yield of about 92 % (Cook, 1976). This means that about 108 kg of coal must be mined to produce, transport and provide (the equivalent of) 100 kg of coal energy.

Coal reserves are scattered throughout the world. Western Europe has about 5 % of the total and the United States about 20 %. Russia, however, is extremely well endowed with nearly 56 % of estimated coal reserves (Cook, 1976).

Adaptation of the world population from oil and gas use to coal use will require many changes in life-style and industrial production methods. The world is indeed fortunate to have coal reserves as a back-up energy resource until new energy sources are discovered and developed.

3 Manipulating Ecosystems for Food Production

Ecosystems

An ecosystem is a network of energy and mineral flows in which the major functional components are populations of plants, animals and microorganisms. These organisms live and perform different specialized functions in the system: i.e. producers, plants; consumers, animals; and reducers, primarily microorganisms. These organisms function to carry out two basic tasks: (1) fixing and utilizing solar energy; and (2) conserving and recycling mineral resources (Fig. 3.1) (Southwood, 1978).

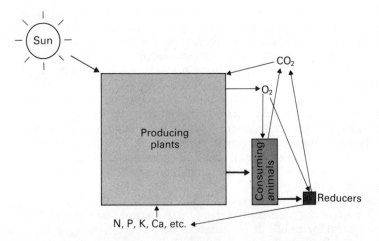

Fig. 3.1 Producing plant-fixed solar energy which is consumed by animals and which is in turn consumed by the reducers. The quantity of energy transferred is schematically diagrammed. Recycling of some of the mineral resources is illustrated.

The collection of solar energy needed to power the entire ecosystem depends directly on the plant population. Plants themselves depend on solar energy to meet their own energy needs. Of the total collected about 25 % is used for respiration, 35 % for building and maintaining structure, and 35 % for reproduction (seeds) (Fig. 3.2).

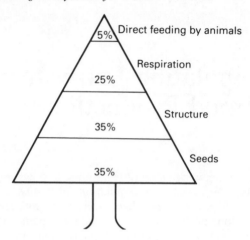

Fig. 3.2 Of the solar energy fixed by crop plants about 25 % is used for respiration, 35 % for building and maintaining the structure, and 35 % for reproduction (seeds). The energy removed by direct feeding is estimated to be about 5 %.

Plants also produce a surplus used by the consumers and reducers. Some animal consumers feed directly upon the plant population but others obtain their energy by feeding on the first-order consumers. In general, the amount of energy removed from the plant population by animals feeding on living plants is small, estimated at about 5 %.

When the plant dies, or the animals that feed on the plant die, the reducers or decomposers obtain a share of the energy originally fixed by the plant population. Reducer populations consist mainly of bacteria, fungi and protozoa. Some invertebrates, such as insects, mites and earthworms, may feed directly on the decaying organic matter, but others feed on the microorganisms that are feeding on this decay.

The reducers serve an essential role in the ecosystem by conserving mineral resources and keeping these essential elements cycling in the system for re-use. If the reducers were unable to recycle the vital elements, the collection and conversion of energy into plant biomass would be limited and eventually cease. A shortage of any one essential element, such as nitrogen, phosphorus, potassium, calcium or sulphur, limits or prevents the normal function of the ecosystem (Fig. 3.1). Hence, the lack of any essential element may be the limiting factor for the entire ecosystem.

A given ecosystem comprises several thousand species of plants, animals and microorganisms. The actual number of species in the network depends upon the boundaries of the ecosystem and the physical environment. The interactions among and between organisms of the system help regulate and stabilize both energy and mineral flows within the complex ecosystems. Further, all ecosystems are interdependent; that is, energy and minerals frequently flow from one ecosystem to another.

Agriculture and the Natural Ecosystem

Neither man, his crops, nor his livestock can exist independently from the other species of the ecosystem. A relatively small number, about 20 major crops and 10 major livestock types, are cultured in agricultural production in the United States and Europe. Contrast this with the estimated 200 000 species of wild plants, animals and microorganisms existing in the United States alone. A majority of these species are necessary for maintenance of the life system of which man and his agriculture are but one part. At present, no one knows how many of the 200 000 species in the ecosystem of the United States can be reduced or eliminated before man's life system is jeopardized. Therefore, we should be cautious, and prevent the degradation or pollution of the environment that might result in either reducing populations or species numbers.

Terrestrial and aquatic plants, including agricultural plants, not only capture sunlight but also renew the oxygen supply and help clean the atmosphere of chemical pollutants. Oxygen and ozone prevent a large percentage of the sun's ultraviolet light from reaching the earth. No terrestrial life could exist on our planet without this protective shield. A small increase in ultraviolet light reaching the earth could have such serious environmental effects as increasing genetic mutations and the incidence of cancer. This is the basis of the recent concerns about the reduction of the ozone layer caused by the use of supersonic aircraft in the upper atmosphere and the release of Freon from aerosols and other sources. Another factor that may become important is the increased use of nitrogen fertilizer, which, when it volatilizes into the atmosphere, may also significantly reduce the protective ozone layer (Schneider, 1975).

Another vital function performed by many species in the natural ecosystem is the breakdown of wastes produced by man, agriculture and the natural system itself. Annually in the United States man alone produces about 100×10^6 tonnes of organic waste. His livestock produce another 1500×10^6 tonnes. Clearly, man would be buried in wastes were it not for the efficient reducing organisms in the natural ecosystem. Bacteria, fungi, protozoa, arthropods and earthworms all help degrade wastes. These reducing organisms help recycle essential minerals for re-use by all members of the ecosystem.

Some organisms improve soil structure while decomposing organic matter. Others, such as earthworms and soil arthropods, help in soil formation. For example, it is estimated that earthworms bring to the surface 2.5 to 63 tonnes of soil castings per hectare (Burges and Raw, 1967) and ants carry up an additional 10 tonnes per hectare (Kevan, 1962).

Pollination of crop and natural plants is another important role of the natural biota of the ecosystem. Without pollination by wild bees, honeybees and other insects, there would be no fruit, and amounts of many vegetables would be reduced. In fact seed production, especially for vegetable and forage crops, would be impossible.

Estimates are that, in New York State, over 8×10^{12} blossoms may be pollinated in a single day by the wild and tame bees combined. An individual honeybee may visit as many as 800 blossoms on a bright sunny day, making about 10 trips and visiting about 80 blossoms on each trip. The total number of honeybee colonies in New York State is estimated at 125 000 with about 10 000 bees per colony. Wild bees, however, pollinate more than half of the blossoms and are vital to the success of seed/fruit production (R. A. Morse, personal communication, 1977).

Biomass

Overall, man and his agricultural system together represent but a small percentage of the total biomass of living matter in the life system. The human biomass in the United States averages about 18 kg ha^{-1}; livestock in the United States averages 76 kg ha^{-1}, outweighing the human population by more than four times (Pimentel *et al.*, 1975).

Crops in the United States contribute slightly more than 20 % of the total plant biomass produced annually. If all crops, pastures, and commercial forests were included, the total would represent about 50 % of the vegetation biomass produced (Pimentel *et al.*, 1978).

But plant biomass is only one part of the total system, for microorganisms are also important contributors. In rich productive soil, fungi and bacteria populations each may weigh (wet) up to 2000 kg ha^{-1}.

Certain natural animal populations are also abundant in favourable habitats. Earthworm populations may weigh up to 1500 kg ha^{-1} and arthropod populations may weigh about 1000 kg ha^{-1}. Thus, compared on a weight basis with man and his livestock, the natural ecosystem significantly dominates in biomass.

Manipulating Agro-ecosystems

One of the earliest views of man's relationship to his ecosphere is found in Genesis 1:28 which says: Be fruitful, and multiply, and replenish the earth, and subdue it. The implication seems clear that man, by employing his energies, could overcome nature. The verse was prophetic; man has been 'fruitful', over-populated he has 'subdued' or modified many sectors of his natural ecosystem with fossil energy.

But it was more than mere population numbers that helped man in his efforts to control nature. The development of tools and machines, coupled with the discovery of such new sources of power as fossil energy and atomic energy, has enabled man to exert tremendous control over his environment. As Forbes (1968) points out, science and technology are the product of the 'interaction between man and environment, based on the wide range of real or imagined needs and desires which guided man in his conquest of Nature.'

In considering the exponential growth of man's technological efforts to populate the earth and alter natural ecosystems, the solemn judgement of Dennis Gabor of the Imperial College of Science and Technology, London, is pertinent: ' . . . exponential curves grow to infinity only in mathematics. In the physical world they either turn around and saturate, or they break down catastrophically. It is our duty as thinking men to do our best towards a gentle saturation instead of sustaining exponential growth, though this faces us with very unfamiliar and distasteful problems' (in Forbes, 1968). Man's alteration of the ecosystem, his unrestrained use of energy, land, water and other vital resources, as well as his tendency to overpopulate, substantiate Gabor's statement.

Man's alteration of the natural ecosystems and use of energy for managing ecosystems directly relates to food production. At this point it is helpful to examine the characteristics of ecosystems and then, in turn, see how these characteristics relate to ecosystem management.

Mature or climax ecosystems are generally complex and contain a wide variety of species. This diversity of species directly contributes to the stability of the system. When natural ecosystems are disturbed, the numbers of species of plants, animals and microorganisms are reduced, and the system becomes relatively simple. After such an alteration, 'successional change' begins and the ecosystem slowly accumulates additional species and gradually a new complex and stable ecosystem evolves.

As natural ecosystems change from simple to complex systems, the quantities of solar energy captured and flowing through the system increase. More energy must be expended to alter a complex ecosystem than to alter a simple ecosystem. Of course, the quantity of energy needed to alter an ecosystem depends upon the extent of the changes to be made. Clearly, less energy is required to change the numbers of one or two species in the ecosystem than to alter the ecosystem and make it a monoculture.

In agricultural production the required energy inputs for manipulation depend directly upon the degree of ecosystem alteration. For instance, when an ecosystem is altered for hay production, the natural vegetation has to be destroyed by cutting the trees and shrubs and removing the stumps; the soil must be turned, limed and fertilized; and finally the hay seed sowed. Large inputs of energy are necessary to make this alteration whether it is done only by manpower or by fuel-powered machinery. Changing an ecosystem to a row crop monoculture such as Brussels sprouts or corn (maize) requires even larger inputs of energy than changing to hay production. For this kind of modification, not only are energy inputs required to destroy the natural vegetation, but additional energy inputs are needed during the growing season to prevent the invasion of weeds and other pests.

Weeds, early successional plant species in nature, will quickly invade a newly planted Brussels sprouts or corn field. The invading weeds must be either uprooted, buried, or chemically destroyed if there is to be optimal crop growth and yield. All these weed control efforts require energy. Inspite of the technology available today, it is impossible to completely exterminate all weeds. Even if it were technically possible, it would be economically and energetically impractical.

In addition to the weeds, there are insects and pathogens that also invade the crop monoculture. The control of these pests requires energy inputs, whether control is accomplished by cultural, environmental or chemical methods.

In summary, natural ecosystems have certain patterns of species development. To alter or change the species structure of an ecosystem, especially to convert it to a monoculture, requires relatively large energy expenditures. The energy investment depends on the crop, growing season and environmental situation.

Interdependency of Land, Water, Labour and Energy in Crop Production

In the management and manipulation of agro-ecosystems, land, water, labour and energy can be substituted for one another within certain limits. The possibility of substituting any one of these factors for another provides some flexibility in the utilization and management of these resources.

In certain areas, for example, crops on 1 ha of high quality land will yield as much as on 2 ha of poorer quality land. On the other hand, the use of more fertilizers and other energy inputs, as well as more labour, may improve the poorer quality land to make it as productive as the high quality land. Thus, land quality, as a factor in crop production, is dependent on available supplies of water, labour and energy.

The impact of soil quality on crop yields and energy use is well illustrated by the environmental problem of soil erosion. Topsoil depths usually average 18–20 cm. For each 2.5 cm of topsoil that is lost from average land, crop productivity is reduced. Each 2.5 cm of soil lost results in an average reduction of 251 kg corn, 161 kg wheat, 168 kg oats or 175 kg soybeans per hectare (Pimentel *et al.*, 1976). Although the reduced productivity of the eroded land can be offset by the use of more fertilizer and other inputs, all these strategies require considerable energy expenditures. In the United States, about 1/3rd of the topsoil from agricultural land has been lost. An estimated 46 litres of fossil energy per hectare in the form of fertilizers and other inputs are expended just to maintain the productivity of the land.

Availability of adequate water supplies often influences the energy inputs and amount of land needed for desired crop production. With ample moisture and heavy fertilizer use, crop plants can be grown densely and high yields result. With limited moisture, however, fewer crop plants can be grown per hectare, less fertilizer can be applied, and crop yields decline.

In some regions, like the wheat-growing section of the state of Washington, lack of moisture necessitates that fields be left fallow for a season. During the fallow year the land collects and stores sufficient moisture to allow a wheat crop to be grown the next year. But, in such an area, overall wheat production is low compared with locations that support yearly harvests.

Adding water through irrigation is a common method of making arid land more productive. Unfortunately, pumping and distributing the water over large areas requires large energy inputs. Therefore, water supply must be considered another interdependent factor in crop production along with energy, arable land and labour.

Increased labour inputs were mentioned earlier relative to crop production on poor quality land compared with production on high quality land. Manpower can be substituted for machinery horsepower in crop production, sometimes with little or no effect on yield. For example, a large proportion of the horsepower in India, Africa, Asia, Oceania, Latin America, UAR and Taiwan is provided by manpower whereas Israel, the United States, Europe, the United Kingdom and Japan are heavily mechanized (Fig. 3.3). Note that

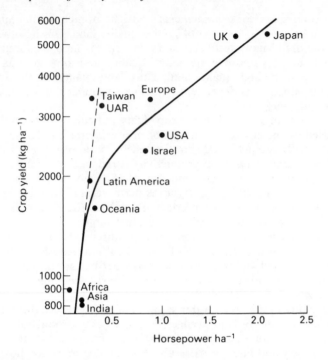

Fig. 3.3   Relationship between crop yields per hectare of cereals, pulses, oil-seeds, sugar crops, potatoes, cassava, onions, and tomatoes and horsepower per hectare in various countries and regions (Asia excludes China) (after Blaxter, 1978).

crop yields for Taiwan and the United Arab Republic are high with minimal horsepower. These data suggest that mechanization and the substitution of manpower with machinery may have little influence on crop yields. More will be said about this later.

Energy, Labour and a Standard of Living

All the operations required in crop culture can be carried out by manpower. However, producing crops by hand requires about 1000 man-hours and only about 1 ha can be managed successfully by one person during a growing season. Under these production conditions only the bare minimum of essential human needs can be attained. This is because the amount of crop yield not needed for food for the farmer and thus considered surplus is extremely small. Only the surplus can be traded for other foods, goods, and services. For this reason, the standard of living achieved from most manpowered systems is relatively low when compared with that possible when mechanization and large inputs of fossil fuel are used in crop production.

Defining low and high standards of living is, at best, imprecise. In general, a relatively high standard of living includes ample food, clothing, housing, autos and numerous other material goods as well as adequate health facilities. However, a high standard of living cannot and should not necessarily be equated with either contentment or happiness.

Fossil energy can replace many man-labour inputs and the use of large supplies of relatively cheap fossil energy is a major reason a high standard of living is possible in the United States, Canada, and Europe. For example, a gallon (3.79 litres) of gasoline sells for about $0.65 in the United States. In 1978, based on a minimum wage of $2.65 per hour, this gallon can be purchased with only 15 minutes of work. However, that one gallon of gasoline in an engine will produce the equivalent of 97 hours of manpower. Thus, one hour of labour at $2.65 will purchase the equivalent of 395 hours of manpower in the form of fossil fuel.

The relative prices of gasoline and labour also affect the price of food. If energy is cheap relative to the price of food, then obviously fossil energy use in food production is an excellent investment. This is true today in the United States. One thousand kilocalories of sweet corn in a can sells for about $0.93 whereas 1000 kcal of gasoline has a value of $0.02. Hence, 1 kcal of sweet corn is worth 47 times more than 1 kcal of gasoline energy.

The relationship of energy expenditure and standard of living can also be clarified by comparing production of corn by labour-intensive and energy-intensive systems. In Mexico, for instance, about 1144 hours of manpower is expended to produce 1 ha of corn by hand (Lewis, 1951). In the United States, under an energy-intensive system, only 12 hours of labour are expended per hectare. In the midwestern United States one farmer can manage success-fully up to 100 ha of corn because he is helped by large fossil fuel inputs that run his mechanized equipment. One farmer producing corn by hand could manage only about 1.5 ha. Assuming the same profit per hectare for each farmer, it is clear that the farmer manag-ing 100 ha will be able to support a higher standard of living.

Thus, fossil energy has helped mankind manipulate ecosystems more effectively and efficiently for food production than ever before, and this has contributed directly to improving the standard of living in many parts of the world.

4 Hunter-gatherers and Early Agriculture

Before the development of agriculture and formal crop culture, wild plants and animals in the natural ecosystem were man's only food supply. This being so, how much wild plant and animal biomass is available for food and how much land must be accessible to the hunter-gatherer to meet his food needs?

The total annual production of plant biomass in the temperate region averages about 2400 kg (dry) per hectare. Under favourable conditions this quantity of plant biomass might support an animal and microorganism biomass of about 200 kg (dry) per hectare per year. The proportions of the total 200 kg of microorganisms, earthworms, arthropods, mammals, birds and reptiles are indicated in Fig. 4.1.

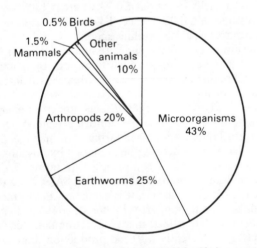

Fig. 4.1 The proportion of the total biomass of 200 kg (dry) present in one hectare that is made up of animals and microorganisms.

Let us assume that a hunter-gatherer requires 2500 kcal per day to meet his energy needs. By harvesting at least 0.1 % of the available animal biomass from 40 ha he will provide himself with 88 kcal per day (32 000 kcal per year) in the form of animal protein. The remaining 2412 kcal per day (880 500 kcal per year) of food energy needed would come from other sources like seeds, nuts, fruits, roots and other plant foods. Assuming that 1 kg of digestible plant material yields 3000 kcal, about 294 kg of plant material would have to be harvested from the 40 ha (7 kg ha^{-1}) to meet the calorie needs. Although obtaining this amount of plant material suitable for food might not be possible in a strictly wooded habitat it should be possible from land containing a mixture of wood, shrub and herb, and a productive stream.

If the food-plant material gathered contains an average of 5 % protein, then a total of 12.2 kg of protein could be harvested per year and amount to about 34 g of plant protein per day. Combining the 34 g of plant protein and the 22 g of animal protein consumed would total 56 g of protein per day in the diet under these optimal conditions. The remaining calories would come from carbohydrate in the plant food and would more than meet the daily energy needs of 2500 kcal per day. Note that the consumption of fat was omitted from the calculations. Fats yielding 9 kcal g^{-1} would add substantially more calories to the daily intake. Except for animal flesh and such plant foods as nuts, the fat content of this diet would undoubtedly be lower than most diets consumed in the world today.

A family of five in a favourable ecosystem would require an estimated 200 ha of habitat from which to gather animal and plant food. This estimate is based on the availability of animal and plant food in an ideal ecosystem, one containing those plants and animals that are most suitable for human consumption.

Others suggest much larger areas are needed by hunter-gatherers. For instance, Clark and Haswell (1970) estimate that at least 150 ha of favourable environmental conditions *per person* are needed to secure an adequate food supply. In a moderately favourable habitat, these scientists estimate that 250 ha per person would be required. These estimates are 4–6 times greater than the model that was discussed earlier as a theoretical possibility.

Under more marginal conditions, such as the cold northwestern Canadian region, about 14 000 ha *per person* are probably necessary to provide a person with about 912 500 kcal of food energy per year (Clark and Haswell, 1970). Land area may range as high as 50 000 ha per person in subarctic lands and in these cold climatic regions, meat and animal products are the predominant foods in the diet. In fact, animal flesh and fat may comprise up to 2/3rds of the food calories consumed.

Plant productivity per hectare in such marginal habitats may average only 10–200 kg per year (Whittaker and Likens, 1975), while animal production may average 2–4 kg ha^{-1} per year. The annual yield of meat for man per hectare may average only 10 g of protein per hectare.

Assuming that 2/3rds of man's calorie intake in such a habitat is animal matter, man could easily consume 102 g of animal protein per day to meet his needed protein intake. The plant products consumed might add another 4 g, bringing the total of protein per day to about 106 g. This is a high protein diet but it is not out of the range of population groups that eat high protein diets. For example, in the United States the average per capita protein consumption is about 101 g per day (USDA, 1976a). To bring calorie intake up to 2500 kcal level, animal fat intake would be higher than the current U.S. diet average of 40–43 % of calories from fat (U.S. Senate, 1977).

Hunters and Gatherers of Food

Hunters and food gatherers probably expend 70–90 % of their energy intake in meeting their food needs. In fact, obtaining food and collecting fuel wood for its preparation usually dominate the activities of these societies.

Since so much human energy is expended in searching for, collecting and transporting food, let us consider the energy required by man for these various activities. The energy expended for these activities, of course, is above that used for the daily basal metabolism, which runs about 45 kcal per hour or 1080 kcal per day (Pyke, 1970). Walking at a rate of about 4 km (2.5 miles) per hour uses about 180 kcal per hour (Table 4.1). If the individual carries a load weighing from 9–23 kg while walking, the energy expended nearly doubles to about 340 kcal per hour (Table 4.1).

Running at 11–13 km (7–8 miles) per hour uses 800–1000 kcal per hour (Table 4.1). If the hunter-gatherer has to walk or run several kilometres hunting or gathering food, the energy expended in food procurement can be relatively large.

Some hunter-gatherer communities exist at a density of 1 person per 15 808 to 31 616 ha (Sahlins, 1972). If only 2/3rds of such a population actively hunts and gathers, then each person must search 47 903 ha (30 square miles) for food. The remaining 1/3rd of the population, consisting of young children and elderly adults, usually does little or no hunting and gathering.

If a hunter-gatherer were to search the 47 903 ha area for food, covering even 58 metre-wide swaths, then he or she would have to travel 8316 km to cover the entire area. This would require that a person walk at a rate of 4 km per hour for 40 hours per week for 52 weeks. Obviously this pace would test the endurance of the most hardy individual and was not done either by early hunter-gatherers

Table 4.1   Energy requirements for various activities (kcal h^{-1}) (from Pyke, 1970).

LIGHT WORK		MODERATE WORK	
Sitting	19	Shoemaking	80–115
Writing	20	Sweeping	85–110
Standing relaxed	20	Dusting	110
Typing	16–40	Washing	125–215
Typing quickly	55	Charring	80–160
Sewing	30–90	Metal working	120–140
Dressing and			
undressing	33	Carpentering	150–190
Drawing	40–50	House painting	145–160
Lithography	40–50	Walking	130–240
Violin playing	40–50		
Tailoring	50–85	VERY HARD WORK	
Washing dishes	60	Stonemasonry	350
Ironing	60	Sawing wood	420
Book-binding	45–90	Coal mining (average	
		for shift)	320
HARD WORK		Running	800–1000
Polishing	175	Climbing	400–900
Joiner work	195	Walking very quickly	570
Blacksmithing	275–350	Rowing very quickly	1240
Riveting	275	Running very quickly	1240
Marching	280–400	Skiing	500–950
Cycling	180–600	Wrestling	1000
Rowing	120–600	Walking upstairs	1000
Swimming	200–700		

nor is it done by hunter-gatherers living in the world today.

Usually hunter-gatherers do not attempt to search their entire area for food. Instead, because they know their territory well, they know approximately where to find food. This greatly reduces the distances that have to be travelled in the search for food. However, even when food location is known, a most distant location would require a trip from one side to the other of the 47 903 ha area or a distance of about 22 km. A round trip across this area would require an expenditure of about 1980 kcal.

The !Kung bushmen who presently inhabit the Dobe area of Botswana, Africa, illustrate the energy economy of a hunter-gatherer society (Lee, 1969; Lee and DeVore, 1976). The population of bushmen that was studied consists of 248 individuals and occupies an area of 2850 square kilometres. Each person requires 10.4 km^2 or 1040 ha for support. Note that this is much less land or only about 3 % of the area for the hunter-gatherers studied by Sahlins.

The habitat in which the !Kung bushmen live is relatively arid with an annual rainfall of only 15–25 cm per year (Lee, 1969; Lee and DeVore, 1976; Marshall, 1976). Permanent watering holes, existing only in locations where the underlying limestone strata have been exposed, provide the only permanent supply of water. During the rainy season, water is also readily available at temporary water holes.

The critical decision facing the bushmen is to locate their camps so that they can obtain both food and water. Since water is the more limiting factor, the bushmen usually locate their camp where they can be assured of obtaining adequate water.

The food gathered by the bushmen consists, by weight, of 33 % mongongo nuts, 37 % meat, and 30 % miscellaneous plant foods (Lee, 1969; Marshall, 1976). On a calorie basis the nuts yield 1200 kcal, meat 768 kcal and other plant foods 172 kcal, totalling a daily energy intake of 2140 kcal. This means that mongongo nuts contribute most of the daily calorie intake of the !Kung bushmen (Fig. 4.2).

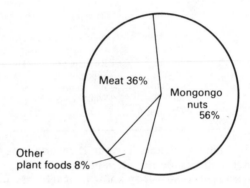

Fig. 4.2 The percentage of various food types that make up the daily diet of the !Kung bushmen (Lee, 1969).

As one might expect, the bushmen prefer to 'collect and eat' the desirable foods that are closest to a water supply. They occupy a camp for a week or a month and literally 'eat their way out of it'. For example, they often locate a camp in the nut forests and 'exhaust the nuts within a 1.6 km (one mile) radius during the first week of occupation, within a 3.2 km (two mile) radius the second week, and within a 4.8 km (three mile) radius the third week' (Lee, 1969).

The energy-cost of obtaining mongongo nuts increases as their distance from camp increases. Specifically, the cost curve rises gradually as the distance of gathering increases from 3 to 19 km (Fig. 4.3). After 19 km, however, the cost curve rises sharply, because then the gatherer must make a 2-day trip instead of a 1-day round

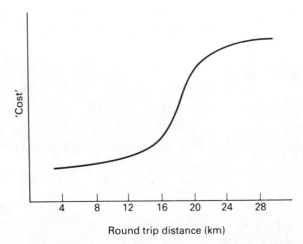

Fig. 4.3 The energy 'cost' of obtaining mongongo nuts at different distances (after Lee, 1969).

trip. In addition, an overnight hike requires the gatherer to carry water and heavier loads during the entire trip.

An alternative to longer food-gathering trips is to eat abundant but less desirable foods that can be found closer to the water holes. During the dry season, when there are fewer water holes, the bushmen use both strategies to maintain their food supplies. The division of labour during these stress periods is such that 'the older, less mobile members of camp stay close to home and collect the less desirable foods while the younger, more active members make the longer trips to the nut forests' (Lee, 1969).

During the rainy season when there are many temporary pools of water, camps are located so both nuts and water are relatively close. During these ideal periods, the gatherers seldom travel more than a 9.7 km (6 mile) round-trip to collect nuts.

The total energy expenditure of a day's average activities that include nut collecting is about 2680 kcal. This energy expenditure can be broken down into activities as shown in Table 4.2.

The energy expended to collect nuts gathered at an average distance of 4.8 km and the energy return from nuts can be calculated from the data of Lee (1969). Walking at 4 km per hour it takes about 1.2 hours to reach the location of the nuts. Walking expends about 180 kcal per hour (Table 4.1). Adding the 45 kcal basal metabolism to this totals 225 kcal per hour and for 1.2 hours, the total energy expended is 270 kcal. Collecting nuts for an estimated 3 hours at 225 kcal per hour results in an estimated 675 kcal expended.

Table 4.2 Input/output analysis of !Kung Bushmen gathering mongongo nuts at a distance of 4.8 km from camp (calculation based on Lee, 1969).

Inputs		
		kcal
Travel to location		
of nuts	4.8 km = 1.2 h	270
Collecting nuts	3 h	675
Return trip to camp	4.8 km carrying	
	12.5 kg nuts = 1.2 h	462
	Subtotal	1407 kcal
Sleep	10.5 h	473
Other activities	8 h	800
	Total	2680 kcal
Outputs		
Nuts shelled, 1.75 kg		10500
Output/input ratio		3.9

The return trip to camp at a distance of 4.8 km also takes about 1.2 hours. However, carrying the load of nuts plus walking requires an expenditure of more calories, an estimated 385 kcal per hour (340 kcal +45 kcal basal metabolism). For 1.2 hours of this activity, 462 kcal is expended.

Then add to this about 473 kcal, which represents basal rate while the bushmen rest and sleep 10.5 hours per day. Considering that other light activities are carried on for 8 hours per day, the energy expenditure is 100 kcal per hour (55 kcal +45 kcal basal metabolism) or an added 800 kcal for the 8 hour period. This brings the total energy expenditure per day to 2680 kcal.

The 12.5 kg of nuts that are collected contain about 2500 nuts. From these 2500 nuts about 1.75 kg of nutmeat is extracted for consumption. The calorie content of the 1.75 kg of nuts is about 10 500 kcal.

With 2680 kcal of inputs to obtain 10 500 kcal of nuts, the basic output/input ratio is 3.9:1. Based on a similar assumption but with the nuts collected 9.6 km distant, then the output/input ratio declines only slightly to 3.3:1 (Table 4.3).

These output/input ratios are based on available data showing that women collect an average 2.2 days per week (range 1.2 to 3.2 days) and that a calculated 23 100 kcal in nuts are obtained per week. This amount provides sufficient food calories for the gatherer (14 296 kcal) as well as a surplus of about 38 %. The surplus 38 % is needed to help feed the children and older dependents who make up the third of the population who do not gather food.

Table 4.3 Input/output analysis of !Kung Bushmen gathering mongongo nuts at a distance of 9.6 km from camp (adapted from Lee, 1969).

Inputs		kcal
Travel to location of nuts	9.6 km = 2.4 h	540
Collecting nuts	3 h	675
Return trip to camp carrying 12.5 kg of nuts	9.6 km = 2.4 h	924
	Subtotal	2139
Sleep	10.5 h	473
Other activities	6 h	600
	Total	3212
Outputs		
Nuts shelled, 1.75 kg		10 500
Output/input ratio		3.3

If the food providers, hunters and gatherers, have to work an average of 2.2 days per week to obtain food, then they have approximately 4.8 days for other activities. These other activities include gathering firewood, moving, constructing shelters (huts) and clothing, caring for children and leisure (Lee, 1969; Marshall, 1976). Observations indicate these bushmen value their leisure and enjoy dancing, visiting other camps, and other social activities.

Early Agriculture

Although we have no accurate written account of the evolution of agriculture, we can logically reconstruct what might have happened. No doubt early agriculture evolved slowly from the less structured societies of food gatherers. We know gatherers brought fruits, vegetables and seeds, including grains, back to camp for consumption. Perhaps some seeds were dropped on the soil in the clearing of the camp, and had the opportunity to grow there. Upon return to the same camp site some time later one can imagine the discovery of the concentration of grains, vegetables or fruits at the site. This probably encouraged some of the more venturesome people to associate seeds with plants and begin to plant seeds themselves.

The relative ease of harvesting such crops compared to random gathering would give encouragement for more plantings. The trend to produce food is thought to have been slow at first, perhaps only a small percentage of the food supply was produced from the gardens, but gradually the percentage increased.

One important step in helping the new seeds to get a good start was the deliberate removal of the existing natural vegetation, including shrubs and trees, which would interfere and compete with crop growth. Burning was the easiest and most common means of clearing the land. Thorough burning not only helped destroy weeds but also added nutrients to the soil. Following burning, the plots were generally clear except for a few large trees and charred stumps.

The seeds were planted by poking holes in the soil with digging sticks and dropping the seeds into the holes. Placing seeds in the cleared ground speeded their germination and subsequent growth so they could compete more successfully with other vegetation considered weeds.

Certainly little or no care was given the early crop plantings. A few months or even a year later the early farmers might return to harvest their crop, or what was left of it. Insects, disease, birds and mammals shared the harvest, and weed competition reduced yield; as many of these same pest species reduce crop yields today.

The next step in the development of early agriculture was to expand the crop plantings sufficiently to produce most of the food supply. With time, as the camps became relatively permanent because food supply was nearby and ample, men and women no longer had to travel to find food. Then too, living close to the plantings allowed a group to claim ownership and protect the plantings from other men as well as from birds, mammals and other pests.

In contrast to agriculture as we know it, early plots were planted and cropped for about two years, then abandoned because production declined as nutrients in the soil became depleted and other problems such as pest outbreaks developed.

Interestingly, this 'cut/burn' or 'swidden' type of agriculture is practiced today in many parts of the world (Ruthenberg, 1971). Swidden agriculture requires that land lay fallow for 10–20 years before it can be re-cleared and planted again. During the long fallow period the soil gradually accumulates the nutrients needed for successful crop production.

Swidden agriculture, when practiced on slopes, can result in severe soil erosion problems. Erosion, of course, is a major problem with all crop production and especially on slopes where the problem is intensified when hilly cropland is left without vegetation (Pimentel *et al.*, 1976). However, soil erosion can be reduced significantly by employing soil conservation practices. For example, logs from some of the trees that are cut can be laid perpendicular to the slope to slow down water runoff (Rappaport, 1968 and 1971). A few trees and their roots left standing in the cleared garden area, plus some partially burned twigs, leaves and other organic matter, all dissipate the energy in raindrops and impede the water runoff that washes away valuable topsoil.

Data from a study of a primitive agricultural society in New
Guinea provide many insights into the energy inputs and outputs of
a swidden type agricultural system (Rappaport, 1968 and 1971). The
ecosystem in New Guinea is a tropical mountainous habitat, with a
rainfall of about 391 cm per year. The relatively steep slopes and
heavy rainfall combined to make soil erosion a problem. These
primitive agriculturists, however, practiced soil conservation,
employing several of the conservation techniques previously
mentioned.

When studied, the village population numbered 204 and occupied
about 830 ha. Only about 364 ha of this land was suitable for crops.
The village annually planted about 19 ha to crops but because some
crops required two years before harvest, about 37 ha were in crops
at any one time. As a result nearly 90 % of the village crop lands
laid fallow each year.

The food of the villagers was almost entirely (99 %) of plant
origin. The primary plants consumed (by weight) were taro, sweet
potato, fruit, leaves, yams, bananas, etc. (Fig. 4.4). The animal
protein came primarily from pigs raised by the villagers, who also
hunted and ate marsupials, snakes, lizards, birds, and insect grubs
found in trees and wood.

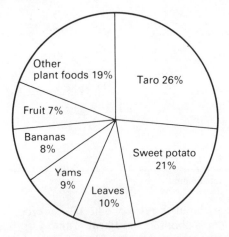

Fig. 4.4 Percentage of the plant materials consumed by the villagers in New
Guinea.

The calorie intake per adult averaged about 2400 kcal per day
and contained about 35 g of protein, mostly of plant origin
(Rappaport, 1968). This protein intake is considered low by FAO
standards that recommend a daily intake of about 40 g of protein
for an adult living under these conditions.

As expected, the production of food in swidden agriculture is labour intensive. The New Guinea villagers worked an estimated 1946 hours per hectare per year in crop production (Rappaport, 1968, 1971). About 42 % of the labour input was for weeding and 15 % was for clearing trees and brush (Table 4.4). Another substantial labour input was for transporting the harvest from the garden plots to the homes for use there. This activity amounted to about 277 hours, but was often viewed as a pleasure because the villagers took pride in harvesting their crop.

Table 4.4   Output/input analysis of New Guinea swidden agriculture for 1 ha of mixed crops that included sweet potato, taro, cassava, yam and banana (after Rappaport, 1968 and 1971).

	Quantity	$kcal\ h^{-1}$	$kcal\ ha^{-1}$
Inputs			
Clearing underbrush	175 h	400	70 000
Clearing trees	68	400	27 200
Fencing garden	84	500	42 000
Weeding and burning	78	300	23 400
Placing soil retainers	44	400	17 600
Planting and all weeding	742	300	222 600
Other maintenance	137	400	54 800
Harvesting	277	300	83 100
Cartage	264	400	145 600
Total	1869 h		686 300
Axe, machete	0.8 kg*		16 860
Seeds, etc.	10 kg*		36 000
			739 160
Outputs			
Crop yield			11 384 462
Output/input ratio			15.4:1

*Estimated as additional inputs.

The total energy input to raise one hectare of crops under this agricultural system is about 739 160 kcal (Table 4.4). Based on an average, yield is about 11.4×10^6 kcal ha^{-1}. The calculated output/input ratio is 15.4:1 (Rappaport, 1968 and 1971).

If we assume that the average per capita consumption per day was 2400 kcal of food, an individual would consume about 876 000 kcal per year. Hence, a one hectare plot would provide sufficient food energy for 13 persons or the 37 ha usually cultivated by the villagers would provide adequate food for the human population of 204.

Interestingly, the villagers consumed only 55 % of the energy value of their crops and fed about 45 % to their pigs (Table 4.4). When this is taken into account the ratio of people to land decreases with the result that only 5.5 persons are sustained per hectare planted.

To feed each pig to slaughter, Rappaport (1971) reported, a total of 4.5×10^6 kcal of feed was necessary over a 10-year period. If we assume that about 65 kcal of feed are required to produce 1 kcal of pork (Pimentel *et al.*, 1975), the return from 4.5×10^6 kcal of feed would be 69 230 kcal of pork. This is only a 1.5 % return on the food energy fed the pigs, or much less than that obtained if the plant foods were consumed directly.

From the 11.4×10^6 kcal harvested from the hectare plot, as mentioned, 45 % (5.1×10^6 kcal) were fed to the pigs (Table 4.4). Based on the calculation that 65 kcal were required to produce 1 kcal of pork for human consumption, the yield from the 5.1×10^6 kcal would be only 78 461 kcal. This 78 461 kcal added to 5.1×10^6 kcal provides a total yield of food energy per hectare of 5.2×10^6 kcal.

There was one advantage to pork production as Rappaport (1968 and 1971) mentions. Keeping pigs was a practical way to store some of the excess food during productive years. Then, when crop harvests were poor, the villagers slaughtered some of the pigs to provide needed additional food.

Another example of the food production by swidden type agriculture is found in a village in the Tepoztlán region of Mexico (Lewis, 1951). The manpower input per hectare for raising the staple-food corn is 1144 hours, compared with 1869 hours in New Guinea for other crops (Table 4.5).

Calculations for total energy output/input for this system are listed in Table 4.5. Basic activities directly related to corn involve an expenditure of 344 800 kcal. Added to this is the 64 350 kcal expended during rest and 85 800 kcal expended for miscellaneous activities. When the energy cost of the axe and hoe and seeds are added, the total energy input to raise a hectare of corn is 548 410 kcal. Balanced against this is a crop yield of 6.8×10^6 kcal; the resulting output/input ratio is 12.6:1. This output/input ratio is only slightly less than the New Guinea swidden agricultural system that had a ratio of 15.4:1.

Thus even primitive societies vary in the energy efficiencies of their methods of securing or producing food. The early hunter-gatherers were probably much like the !Kung bushmen of today who have an average output/input ratio of about 4:1, under ideal conditions.

Somewhat more organized agricultural production systems like those of the villagers in New Guinea and Mexico have more favour-

Table 4.5   Energy inputs in corn production in Mexico using swidden agriculture (after Lewis, 1951).

	Quantity ha^{-1}	kcal h^{-1}	kcal ha^{-1}
Inputs			
Clearing with machete and axe	320 h	400	128 000
Fencing with poles	96	400	38 400
Burning	64	300	19 200
Seeding	96	300	38 400
Reseeding	32	300	9 600
Weeding	240	300	72 000
Transporting corn	80	400	3 200
Shelling corn	120	300	36 000
Total work	1144 h		344 800
Rest	1430 h		64 350
Other activities	858		85 800
Axe and hoe	0.8 kg*		16 860
Seeds	10.4 kg*		36 600
Total			548 410
Outputs			
Crop yield	1944 kg		6 901 200
Output/input ratio			12.5:1

*Estimated as additional inputs.

able energy ratios of 12 to 15:1. In addition, less land per person fed is necessary in those systems where more crop culture was practiced.

5 Early Livestock Systems and Animal Power

Role of Animals in Society

Throughout his history, man has depended upon animals for food, power and companionship. He has even worshipped animals such as the tiger, leopard and lion. Even today, animals seem to symbolize a special power. For example, one can purchase a Jaguar, Cougar or Bobcat automobile, or have the gasoline attendant 'put a tiger in the tank.' The major role of animals, however, has been to provide food and power to help man cultivate his crops, build his shelters and transport his supplies.

All available evidence tends to confirm that man is an omnivore. He has the capacity to use as food not only a wide variety of plant materials, but also animal flesh. The relative proportion of plant to animal food consumed varies with cultural habits, availability of food and personal preference.

Early Animal Herding

Early civilizations depended upon both animal husbandry and crop culture to supplement hunting and gathering of wild food. The first animals man kept as a source of food were chickens, ducks, pigs, rabbits, sheep, goats, cattle, camels, donkeys and llamas. These animals provided meat, fat, milk and blood for energy and protein as well as other major nutrients.

Animal husbandry probably began when a hunter carried his prey's young back to camp. There, fed and protected, the animals thrived and could be killed when man needed additional food. Later on, some of the captive animals were tamed and allowed to breed and reproduce. Eventually, the numbers in captivity were sufficient not only to provide immediate food, but also to breed, thus ensuring a continuing, relatively stable food supply.

Certainly herding was more efficient and dependable than nunting because it greatly reduced the time and energy man had to spend in pursuit of wild animals. Further, the work involved in herding was easily done by women and children, thus freeing the men to do other tasks necessary for the survival of the community.

In addition, maintaining herds of sheep, goats, cattle and camels was a dependable way for man to store surplus food produced during highly successful crop years. In periods of poor environmental conditions, when plant crop yields were low, the livestock were an available food supply.

The stabilization of food supply through animal husbandry was even more helpful to those humans who were attempting to survive in marginal habitats. In severely wet, dry, cold or mountainous environments, crop production is difficult, unpredictable, and sometimes nearly impossible. Moreover, in many of these habitats, the species of tolerant grasses and other forages that grow well are not suitable for human food. Fortunately, these plants are suitable food for livestock, which convert them into animal food that man can use.

The herding carried out by the Dodo tribe of northeast Uganda illustrates the advantage of husbanding livestock in marginal habitats (Deshler, 1965). During the Deshler study, the Dodo tribe numbered about 20 000 and herded about 75 000 head of Zebu cattle over an area of about 780 000 ha, or approximately 10 ha per head of cattle.

The human population density was low, about one per 390 ha making the ratio of cattle to people about 38:1. Based on a biomass comparison, the cattle outweighed the human population by more than 187:1.

The habitat in which the Dodos live is bleak, consisting primarily of thorn scrub and perennial grasses, and having an average rainfall of between 45 and 62 cm per year. In addition to herding, the Dodos culture sorghum, which has ample yields during good rainfall years. Unfortunately, low rainfall years also are common in that part of Uganda, making sorghum an unreliable food resource. When the sorghum harvest is poor, the cattle provide needed food in the form of milk, blood and meat. In addition, cattle are traded for money, which is used to purchase sorghum when local supplies are inadequate.

The milk yield from the 75 000 head of cattle is estimated at 2500×10^6 kcal, meat at 2300×10^6 kcal, and blood at 630×10^6 kcal annually (Pimentel *et al.*, 1975; Westoby *et al.*, 1978). To produce this total of 5430×10^6 kcal of food energy, the cattle are fed no grain but only pasture forage that is unsuitable for human consumption. Forage consumption is estimated at 8 kg per animal per day (Pimentel *et al.*, 1975; Westoby *et al.*, 1978).

Little or no fossil fuel is used by the Dodos in managing this livestock and work is done by manpower. With the Dodo population estimated at 20 000, and assuming that 40 % of the males work 56 hours per week and 40 % of the females work 7 hours per week in herding, the estimate is that 34 man hours per hectare of grazing land per year is invested in managing this livestock system.

The yield in animal protein is 0.7 kg ha^{-1} annually with an input of 34 man hours, as mentioned. The energy input per working hour is calculated to be 250 kcal per hour. Assuming 8 hours of work with an expenditure of 250 kcal per hour, 10 hours rest at 45 kcal per hour, and 6 hours of other activities at 100 kcal per hour for the males who work at herding, then the daily per capita energy input in caring for the Zebu cattle is 3050 kcal.

With an estimated 8000 working males caring for the cattle, this totals 24.4 $\times 10^6$ kcal per day, or 8900 $\times 10^6$ kcal per year. In measuring the energy input of the females, only one hour work per day is counted because most of their time is spent caring for the sorghum plots (Deshler, 1965). When the annual female input in herding of 730 $\times 10^6$ kcal is added to the male input, the total input for herding the cattle is 9600 $\times 10^6$ kcal.

With 5430 $\times 10^6$ kcal of animal protein produced and an energy input of 9600 $\times 10^6$ kcal, the output/input ratio is only 0.54:1 or about 2 calories input per output calories. Based on the animal protein produced, the Dodo could not maintain themselves only on livestock. However, as mentioned, sorghum is a staple food of the Dodo (Deshler, 1965). Thus, the livestock protein produced is used to supplement the sorghum raised or purchased.

The culture of livestock by the Dodo tribe illustrates the important role that livestock play in providing food for man in this ecological system. First, the livestock effectively convert forage growing on the marginal habitat into food (milk, meat, blood) suitable for man. Second, the livestock population serves as a stored food resource. In addition, the cattle herds are valuable resources that can be traded for sorghum grain during years of inadequate crop yields.

Animal Power as an Energy Source

For most of the time man has inhabited the earth, his prime source of power has been his own body. He transported himself and carried goods, tilled his land, planted seeds, cultivated and harvested his crops, ground cereals, hunted animals and protected himself from the predation of animals and other men.

Early additional sources of power were contributed by other humans who served as slaves and by animals that were tamed. The hunting and gathering societies were helped when an extra food gatherer or hunter could join in the task of securing food. Likewise, the manpower intensiveness of primitive agriculture increased both the need for and usefulness of slave and animal labour.

In hunting, one or two extra persons could guide wild game to a concealed hunter, and an added hunter could help in the exhausting task of tracking and killing the wounded animal. Usually the killing of large animals required the skill and manpower of several hunters. Even after the kill, considerable energy was expended when the carcass was transported back to camp, often a long distance. Thus an extra human back or additional manpower was a distinct asset after a successful kill.

The slave or extra hunter, of course, would have to be fed. A hunter with an additional helper, however, could more than supply both their needs while securing enough food for the camp. In this way, a slave provided a greater return in energy than the energy input required for his maintenance.

Along with slave power, animal power slowly evolved as an additional source of power for man. Young animals captured in the wild could be tamed and later used as a means of transporting goods and people. At first these animals were probably used to carry collected food or animal carcasses back to camp. In addition, nomadic groups used animals to move their belongings to new campsites.

With time, many kinds of animals have served as beasts of burden. Records show one of the first used was the donkey, found in Egypt about 3000 B.C. (Leonard, 1973) and later in Mesopotamia about 1800 B.C. (Zeuner, 1963). Agriculture was already an important activity of these societies, and animals were used to transport the harvest from the field to the village. Gradually, aided by an improved system of transport, trade between villages developed.

As early as 2500 B.C., cattle, including oxen and water buffalo, were used as beasts of burden and to draw ploughs (Leonard, 1973). The use of animal power to draw a plough and cultivate the soil was an immense breakthrough in agricultural production. Tremendous quantities of energy and about 400 hours of heavy labour were expended when man worked alone to turn a hectare of soil for planting. With one hour of ox power substituting for 3–5 hours of manpower, the time and man-energy requirement was drastically reduced.

The next step was the use of horses, a significant improvement over oxen because horses move faster. Best estimates are that horses inhabited Asia but were probably not domesticated until about 3000 B.C. (Lee, 1955). As with oxen, horses were first used to transport goods and people, and later to help man till his fields. Other animals that have been used to carry man and his goods include the camel, llama, goat and even the dog.

About 3000 B.C. the invention of the wheel made possible a tremendous increase in the efficiency of energy used in transport

(Lee, 1955). The use of the wheel doubled the load of goods that could be transported without any added energy input either by man or other animals. This surplus or extra energy was then available for use in other ways and undoubtedly helped man improve his standard of living.

In addition, the wheel led to improved efficiency in other food-related processes such as grinding cereals. Grinding grain by hand was slow and tedious. At first animals powered the early grinding wheels, but later man found ways to harness wind and water for power. Of course, wind and water power were significantly more efficient than animal power because their use did not require food for maintenance.

Although wind and water power are more efficient for grinding grain than either animal or manpower, there are many tasks for which manpower is the most efficient energy source. This can be illustrated by analyzing the energy inputs in tilling soil and applying herbicides. A man using a heavy hoe to till one hectare of soil for planting needs about 400 hours to complete the task or forty 10-hour work days (Lewis, 1951). If we assume 400 kcal are expended per hour for this heavy work and the man works a 10-hour day, this amounts to 4000 kcal expended per day for the work. To this must be added the energy required to maintain the worker for the other 14 hours of each day. It is assumed that he rests for 10 hours at 45 kcal per hour and that his other 4 hours of activities of eating, etc. require 100 kcal per hour. Hence, total energy expenditure for one man is 4850 kcal per day. When this daily energy expenditure is multiplied by 40 days of work, the total energy input is about 194 000 kcal (Table 5.1). An added 6000 kcal input is required for construction and maintenance of the heavy hoe. Thus, the total energy input to till one hectare by manpower alone is about 200 000 kcal.

In contrast, oxen, small hand tractors and 50-hp tractors all require greater total energy expenditures in spite of the fact all require less time to. complete the task. For example, an oxen pair takes only 65 hours but expends almost 50 % more energy, than manpower-tilling does (Table 5.1). This is because the oxen must be fed and need a man to guide them as they work.

Likewise, 6-hp and 50-hp tractors use much less time, 25 and 4 hours respectively, to till one hectare that requires 400 hours of manpower (Table 5.1). But the total energy input is far greater than that for either man or oxpower because of the large kcal input of petroleum needed to run the engines.

Considering the current prices of fuel, hay and labour in all countries, it is generally more economical to till the soil with either machinery or oxen than with manpower. The reason is that man-

Table 5.1 Comparison of energy inputs for tilling 1 ha of soil by manpower, oxen, 6-hp tractor and 50-hp tractor.

Tilling unit	Required hours	Machinery input (kcal)	Petroleum input (kcal)	Manpower input (kcal)	Oxen Power input (kcal)	Total input (kcal)
Manpower	400	6000	0	194 000	—	200 000
Oxen (pair)	65	6000	0	31 525	260 000[a]	297 525
6-hp tractor	25	191 631[d]	237 562[b]	12 125	—	441 318
50-hp tractor	4	245 288[e]	306 303[c]	2400	—	553 991

(a) Each ox is assumed to consume 20 000 kcal of feed per day. (b) An estimated 23.5 litres of gasoline used. (c) An estimated 30.3 litres of gasoline used. (d) An estimated 191 631 kcal machinery was used in the tillage operation. (e) An estimated 245 288 kcal machinery was used in the tillage operation.

power is the most costly power. If prices of fuels rise, machinery may no longer be quite the energy bargain it is today.

Tilling the soil is an example of extremely heavy work for both man and tractor. To keep the relative efficiencies of man and tractor in perspective, a comparison of energy inputs in applying herbicides is helpful. A man takes about 3 hours to hand spray 1 ha with herbicide. The energy for this manpower was estimated at 300 kcal per hour or a total of 900 kcal. Adding 8 kcal for the construction and maintenance of the hand sprayer brings the total input for the spraying task to 908 kcal (Table 5.2).

Table 5.2   Comparison of energy inputs for spraying herbicide on 1 ha by manpower and using a 50-hp tractor.

Spraying unit	Required hours	Machinery input (kcal)	Petroleum input (kcal)	Manpower input (kcal)	Total input (kcal)
Manpower	3.0	8[a]	0	900	908
50-hp tractor	0.7	21 463[b]	30 327[c]	210	52 000

(a) An estimated 8 kcal of machinery used in the spraying operation. (b) An estimated 21 463 kcal of machinery used in the spraying operation. (c) An estimated 3 litres of gasoline used.

The 50-hp tractor using a power driven sprayer requires only 0.7 hours to spray a hectare. The gasoline input is estimated at 3 litres or 30 327 kcal energy and the manpower input for 0.7 hour total was assumed to be 210 kcal. An added 21 463 kcal energy is expended for the construction and maintenance of both tractor and sprayer. Thus, the total energy input for tractor spraying is about 52 000 kcal or about 57 times greater than for hand spraying (Table 5.2). It is obvious that using a 50-hp tractor for this task is energy wasteful and, in fact, the tractor is overpowered for such light work. The tractor and sprayer weigh 5–6 tonnes and a large input of energy is needed to move these weights over the field.

When only dollar cost is considered, applying herbicide by hand would be more economical than employing a tractor. Thus, in a country where farm wages might be as low as $0.50 per hour, applying herbicide by hand would cost an estimated $1.30, whereas using the tractor would cost an estimated $1.88 (F.g. 5.1). Hand spraying becomes increasingly expensive as the hourly wage for labourers increases.

In these comparisons, nothing has been said about the type of energy used, and this is a vital factor to consider. The man needs food, and the tractor depends upon petroleum, whereas the ox consumes forage, a plant product that man cannot use for food. In

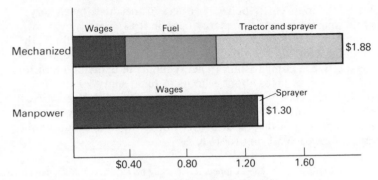

Fig. 5.1 Economic costs of applying herbicide in a developing country.

many regions, forage can be considered a free energy source. Forage growing along paths, waterways, and similar areas that do not compete with croplands can be fed the oxen or other draft animals. Also, straw left from the harvest of rice or similar grain crops can be fed and utilized by animals. Hence, the energy cost of maintaining an ox might be minimal to the small farmer.

Draft animals such as water buffalo have additional advantages because they provide milk and meat as well as power. With animal protein foods at a premium in some developing countries, this supply of animal protein is of great nutritional value.

Many nations have replaced draft animals with tractors and other machinery. For example, when the United States was first settled in 1620, manpower was the prime power source for work, but by 1776, an estimated 70 % of the power was supplied by animals, and 20 % by men (Cook, 1976).

By 1850, animal power had declined to 53 % and manpower to 13 % (Cook, 1976) (Fig. 5.2). About 100 years later in 1950, animal power and manpower declined to only about 1 %, while fossil-fuel-driven engines provided 95 % of the power. Thus, a dramatic change has taken place that has far-reaching consequences as man continues to consume ever-increasing quantities of nonrenewable resources – the fossil fuels.

Animal Food Consumption Patterns

All evidence concerning the eating patterns of man tends to confirm he is an omnivore. Although an omnivore, the specific diets range from one composed primarily of plant material and protein to one primarily of animal material and protein.

Throughout history animals, either hunted or husbanded, have been valued by man for food, in spite of the fact that the majority

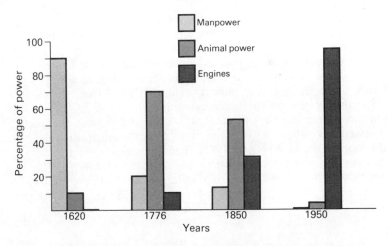

Fig. 5.2 The percentage of power provided by manpower, animal power and engines during various periods in U.S. history (sources: 1620 estimated, 1776, 1850, and 1950 from Cook, 1976).

of mankind has always had to depend primarily on plant materials for energy and other nutrients. Even today most of the world population lives on about 2100 kcal per capita per day and obtains most of its food energy and protein from grains and legumes (PSAC, 1967). Examples are numerous. For instance, one of the unique human diets on record was consumed in Ireland during the 19th century. At this time the Irish people relied primarily on potatoes for both calories and protein, and daily consumed about 4.5 kg of potatoes and about half a litre of milk (Connell, 1950). These two foods provided about 3852 kcal and 64 g of protein per day, of which 45 g were from the potatoes.

Or recall the diet of the New Guinea villagers studied by Rappaport (1968), who consumed primarily plant foods (Fig. 4.4). Indeed, about 99 % of their calories came from plant material.

A recent example is the dietary regime of 12 rural villages in southern India, where the average daily consumption per family member was between 210 and 330 g of rice and wheat, 140 ml of milk, and 40 g of pulses and beans (Tandon *et al.*, 1972). This provided about 1500 kcal and 48 g of protein per day with the major share of both calories and protein coming from plants.

In Central America, where corn (maize) is the staple food, labourers commonly consume about 500 g of corn per day (E. Villagrán (1975), personal communication). Consumed with the corn is about 100 g of black beans per day and together these provide about 2118 kcal and 68 g of protein daily. The corn and beans complement each other by providing the essential amino acids that are needed for humans. Additional food energy is obtained from other plant and animal products that are also eaten.

A sharp contrast to all these examples is found in the United States, where the daily protein intake is about 101 g, of which 2/3rds, or about 69 g, is of animal origin (USDA, 1976b).

Specifically, the per capita animal and animal protein consumption in the United States is one of the highest in the world, although this pattern is typical of many highly industrialized nations in Europe (OECD, 1974). In 1975, annual per capita meat consumption was 115 kg, or about 320 g per day (USDA, 1976b and 1977a). Beef is the meat eaten in largest amount (Fig. 5.3). In addition, the annual per capita consumption is 285 eggs (36 kg) and about 130 kg of milk (USDA, 1976b).

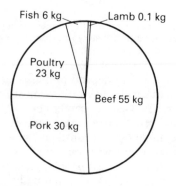

Fig. 5.3 Annual meat consumption per person in the United States (USDA, 1976b).

Although mammals and mammal products like milk and cheese dominate the animal materials consumed by man, a great variety of other animal material is also eaten. Included are many kinds of birds and their eggs, ranging all the way from large ostrich eggs to tiny birds like the English sparrow. Often the small birds, plucked of feathers and cooked on skewers, are eaten whole, bones and all (Laycock, 1966).

Eggs are eaten in a variety of ways: raw, cooked, incubated, preserved and pickled. Some of the uniquely prepared eggs are the Chinese or 'century' eggs and Philippine 'balut'. The century eggs are preserved in lime, coated with clay, and buried for long periods of time. As the name implies, century eggs will keep for many years. After preservation the white portion of the egg is a black gelatinous material and the yolk becomes a dark green to black colour.

'Balut', the egg delicacy of the Philippines, is a duck egg that has been fertilized and incubated for about 17 days. Considering that on day 21 a young duckling normally would hatch from the egg, at day 17 a fairly well-developed young duckling is present within the shell. The egg is boiled, and eaten hot or cold. Most Westerners find eating a partially developed duckling something of a feat the first time.

Fresh and saltwater fish and their eggs are also favourite foods when supplies are easily accessible and ample. Fish are prepared in many different ways – raw, salted, smoked, dried, boiled, baked, broiled, as well as by combinations of these processes.

Arthropods like shrimp, crayfish, lobster, and their close relatives, the insects, are eaten in many parts of the world. In Europe and the United States, shrimp, crayfish, and lobster are some of the most highly valued and highly priced foods, yet their smaller insect relatives are considered unacceptable. In fact, in the United States various government regulations have been established to insure that insects and insect parts are kept to a minimum in food (FDA, 1974). The small herbivorous insects that are present in U.S. foods despite the regulations include aphids, thrips and dipterans. Of the insects that are intentionally used as food, are the large insects such as grubs, locusts and grasshoppers (Pimentel *et al.*, 1977).

Lizards, snakes, snails and frogs are also eaten by many people. In fact, some cultures consider frogs and snails a delicacy. Lizards and snakes are also eaten and are reported to have excellent palatability characteristics.

Nutritional Quality of Protein Foods

One of the important considerations in evaluating the relative value of plant and animal protein sources is their nutritional content. A broad comparison shows, for instance, that one cup of cooked dried beans (190 g) is quite similar to an 85 g serving of cooked ground beef in the amounts of protein, iron and important B vitamins (USDA, 1975c). Further, the beans contain no fat, cholesterol and no vitamin B_{12}.

Although the amount or quantity of protein in average servings of these foods is similar, the nutritional quality of the protein is different. By quality it is meant both the kind and amounts of the so called 'nutritionally essential' amino acids that make up proteins. Animal proteins contain the eight essential amino acids in optimum amounts and in forms utilizeable by humans for protein synthesis. For this reason, animal proteins are considered high-quality proteins.

By comparison, plant proteins contain lesser amounts of some of the essential amino acids and are judged to be lower in nutritional quality than animal sources. In addition, some plant proteins are deficient in one or more essential amino acid. For example, cereal grains as a group are relatively low in lysine while legumes, such as dried beans and peas are relatively low in methionine but have ample amounts of lysine present. Fortunately, it is possible to combine plant proteins to complement the amino-acid deficiencies. Thus, when cereal and legume proteins are eaten together, the 'balance' in the amino-acid supply and the mixture of protein are of better quality than that provided by either eaten alone (NAS, 1974b).

More attention and thought must be given to planning a diet that is either limited in or entirely devoid of animal protein. According to Register and Sonneberg (1973), a variety in choice of plant foods is of prime importance in achieving a nutritionally balanced diet under such constraints. Further, because B_{12}, an essential vitamin, is not found in plant foods, this must be taken as a supplement. The diets of nutritionally vulnerable groups like infants, growing children and pregnant women often require additional nutritional supplements when a strict plant food regime is undertaken. Individuals in these categories often find it difficult to consume the quantity of plant material necessary to provide such essential nutrients as calcium and iron.

Another advantage of animal products over plant products as food for man and especially children is the greater concentration of food energy per unit weight compared with plant material. This can be illustrated with sweet corn and beef. To obtain 375 kcal of food energy from sweet corn one has to consume 455 g, while the same amount of food energy (375 kcal) is found in only 140 g of beef. Thus, beef has more than three times as much food energy per unit weight as sweet corn.

6 Energy Use in Livestock Production

Production Systems

The amount of energy expended in livestock production systems depends not only on the animal but the type of feed. Animals vary in the efficiency with which they convert plant energy and protein into animal protein foods. In addition, they vary in their ability to utilize different plant foods.

On a worldwide basis, about 25 % (30 ×10⁶ tonnes) of the protein consumed is animal protein (Fig. 6.1 and Table 6.1). Best estimates are that more than 60 % of this livestock protein comes from animals fed grasses and forages that cannot be utilized by man. The remainder comes from livestock fed plant and animal protein that is suitable food for man. Specifically the 50 ×10⁶ tonnes of plant and animal protein suitable for man yield only an estimated 13 ×10⁶ tonnes of the livestock protein. This means that, in addition to large amounts of forage, 4 kg dry plant protein suitable for human consumption is converted into 1 kg animal protein. Obviously this plant to animal protein conversion is relatively inefficient when compared with direct consumption of plant proteins by humans.

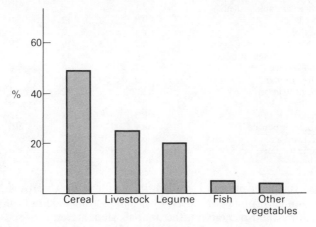

Fig. 6.1 The percentage of protein available to mankind worldwide.

In the United States and other highly industrialized countries where high protein/high animal protein diets are typical, intensive livestock production systems are maintained to supply the large quantities of animal products.

Basic to maintaining these systems is the use of large amounts of cereal grains which, though useful to animals, are also nutritious human food. In the United States, for example, an estimated 1300 kg of grain (excluding exports) is produced per person per year (USDA, 1976a). Of this man eats only 110 kg and the remaining 1190 kg are fed to livestock. Or put another way, in addition to forage consumed, an estimated 26×10^6 tonnes of plant and animal protein quite suitable for human consumption are fed to animals who in turn produce 6×10^6 tonnes of animal protein (Table 6.1). A relatively large amount of this plant protein comes from various grains and legumes. As a result, on the average, for every 5 kg of plant and fish protein fed only 1 kg of animal protein is produced.

Table 6.1 Estimated plant and animal protein produced (million tonnes) and consumed by man and livestock in the world (Pimentel *et al.*, 1975).

Item	USA	Worldwide		
		1975	2000	Alternative for 2000
Total cereal protein produced	17.0	95	166	134
Fed to livestock	15.5	38	49	0
Available to man	1.5	57	117	134
Total legume protein produced	9.3	30	50	36
Fed to livestock	9.0	6	8	0
Available to man	0.3	24	42	36
Total other vegetable protein produced	0.8	6	12	9
Fed to livestock	0.1	1	2	0
Available to man	0.7	5	10	9
Total livestock protein produced	6.0	33	43	25
Fed to livestock	0.7	3	4	0
Available to man	5.3	30	39	25
Total fish protein produced	1.0	9	12	12
Fed to livestock	0.8	3	4	0
Available to man	0.2	6	8	12
Total protein produced	34.1	173	283	216
Fed to livestock	26.1	51	67	0
Available to man	8.0	122	216	216

Whenever plant protein is cycled through animals to provide high quality animal protein the 'costs' of production include not only the plant calories and protein fed the animals slaughtered for food but also that fed the breeding herd. More will be said about both these

'costs' in the following discussion of the production of various livestock products.

Milk production

Of all the animal protein products produced, milk is the most
efficiently produced, based on the proportion of plant protein converted into animal protein (Table 6.2). In several New York State
dairy herds, about 60 kg of milk protein is produced from about
190 kg of protein, a conversion rate of 31 %. Of the 190 kg of plant
protein that is fed the cattle and replacement heifers, about half is
from grains suitable for human consumption, while 90 kg is forage.

On an energy basis, about 7.0×10^6 kcal of feed energy is used by
a dairy cow to produce 236 000 kcal (50 kg) of milk protein, or
about 30 kcal of feed energy per kcal of milk protein produced.
These results agree favourably with those of Reid (1970) who
reports a 28:1 ratio for milk protein production.

The dairy cow is considered relatively efficient in converting feed
protein into milk protein because, compared to other animals, it has
a fairly long productive period of 4–5 years. The cost of the
replacement heifer is therefore relatively small; from 1/4 to 1/5th of
a heifer has to be fed per year as the replacement. Contrast this
with beef production, for which both the beef animal and its mother
must be fed all year.

Additional considerations in the production of milk are the
energy expenditures of tractors, trucks, manure movers and other
equipment. The fossil energy input for feed and animal production
requires about 36 kcal per kcal of milk protein produced. This is
higher than the 20:1 ratio reported by Leach (1976) for milk protein
production in the United Kingdom. Based on labour inputs, 2.6 kg
milk protein is produced for every man-hour of work.

Egg production

Next to milk production, egg protein is the most efficiently
produced animal protein. An estimated 27 % of the plant protein fed
the chickens is converted into egg protein; that is, about 180 kg of
egg protein is produced from about 670 kg of feed protein. An
important consideration, however, is that most of the plant protein
fed to chickens also is suitable for human consumption.

An estimated 14.4×10^6 kcal of feed energy are fed the chickens
to produce 188 kg of egg protein (Table 6.2). Thus, about 20 kcal of
feed energy is fed per kcal of egg protein produced.

The total fossil energy input in this system is about 9.6×10^6 kcal,
including energy expended in growing feed and maintaining the

Table 6.2 Analysis of vegetable protein production per hectare for various crops in the United States and elsewhere requiring different amounts of labour and energy (after Pimentel et al., 1975).*

Crop	Crop yield in protein (kg)	Crop yield (kg)	Crop yield in food energy (10^6 kcal)	Fossil energy input for production (10^6 kcal)	Labour (man-hours)	kcal fossil energy input/ kcal protein output
Alfalfa[a]	710	6451 (dry)	11.4	2.694	9	0.95
Soybeans[b]	640	1882	7.6	5.285	15	2.06
Brussel sprouts[a]	604	12 320	5.5	8.492	60	3.51
Potatoes[a]	524	26 208	20.2	8.907	60	4.25
Corn[a]	457	5080	17.9	6.644	22	3.63
Corn silage[a]	393	30 200	24.1	5.493	25	3.49
Rice[a]	388	5796	21.0	15.536	30	10.01
Dry beans[a]	325	1457	5.0	4.478	15	3.44
Oats[a]	276	1900	7.4	2.978	6	2.70
Wheat[a]	274	2284	7.5	3.770	7	3.44
Hay[a]	200	5000 (dry)	8.6	3.115	16	3.89
Corn (Mexico)[c]	175	1944	6.8	0.053	1144	0.08
Rice (Philippines)[c]	111	1654	6.0	0.582	576	1.31
Wheat (India)[c]	99	821	2.7	0.256	615	0.65
Sorghum (Sudan)[c]	99	900	3.0	0.079	240	0.20
Cassava (Tanga)[c]	58	5824 (dry)	19.2	0.016	1284	0.07

(a) Data from Pimentel, 1976. (b) Data from Pimentel, 1976. The inputs include about 1.1 million kcal for processing the beans to make them edible for livestock. (c) Data from Pimentel et al., 1974. * Some yield and energy input values may differ from yield and input values presented in Chapters 7 and 8. Values in this table are values for the United States.

flocks. Comparing fossil fuel inputs, the ratic of 13 kcal input to 1 kcal egg protein produced is 1/3rd that of milk protein production. Thus, chickens are relatively efficient converters of both feed and fossil energy into egg protein. This is because a chicken is productive for about one year and a replacement hen requires only 3–4 months of feed before it too begins egg production.

Broiler production

Although broiler protein production is similar to egg protein production, it is less efficient. Only an estimated 18 % of the plant protein fed broilers is converted into broiler protein; i.e. about 120 kg of broiler protein is produced from feeding about 650 kg of feed protein. In addition, like egg production most of the plant protein fed the broilers is grain, suitable for human consumption.

Almost 8.9 million kcal of feed energy is consumed by the broilers to produce the 116 kg of broiler protein (Table 6.2). This means about 19 kcal of feed energy is expended per kcal of broiler protein produced, and is quite similar to the 20:1 ratio for egg protein production.

The feed energy efficiency in broiler protein production is due to the following factors: (1) the hen produces a large number of off-spring (231 eggs); (2) only 10 weeks are necessary to feed a broiler up to the marketable weight; and (3) broilers make efficient use of their feed.

In evaluating the fossil fuel input/output ratio, the 22:1 for broiler production is nearly twice that for egg production but lower than that for milk.

Pork production

Compared with milk production, pork production is less than 1/3rd as efficient in converting plant protein into animal protein (Table 6.2). Hogs convert only about 9 % of the plant protein fed to them into pork protein; i.e. only 65 kg of pork protein is produced from 690 kg of feed protein given to the hogs.

Although much of the protein fed to the hogs is suitable for human consumption, they can be maintained satisfactorily on food wastes, such as table wastes or garbage. They can also eat surplus foods produced from gardens during the growing season. Pastured hogs often will root out and eat vegetation and various roots and they have been known to feed on acorns and certain other plant foods that are considered marginal for human consumption.

An estimated 17.0×10^6 kcal in feed are consumed by hogs to produce the 65 kg of pork protein. This is an expenditure of about 65 kcal of feed energy per kcal of pork protein produced and is somewhat greater than Reid's (1970) estimate of 51:1.

The fossil energy input is calculated to be about 35 kcal feed energy per kcal of pork produced. This ratio is about average for the animal protein products.

One of the major advantages of husbanding hogs, rather than cattle or sheep, is that hogs produce litters ranging from 6 to 10 piglets. This substantially reduces the number of animals in the breeding herd that must be fed and maintained to supply the young that will be reared solely for meat. Maintaining a breeding herd has high costs in both feed and husbandry energy.

Grain/grass beef production

In the feedlot system, the protein fed to the beef and breeding stock consists of about 42 % forage with the remainder being grain. Feedlot or grain/grass beef protein production has a feed protein conversion efficiency of only 6 % (Table 6.2). About 50 kg of animal protein is produced from about 790 kg of plant protein feed fed to these animals.

An estimated 25×10^6 kcal are fed to these beef animals to produce the 50 kg of beef protein. This amounts to about 122 kcal of feed energy consumed per kcal of beef protein produced and agrees favourably with Reid's (1970) reported ratio of 123:1.

The fossil energy input to produce the protein output is calculated to be about 78 kcal of fossil energy expended for one kcal of beef protein produced. This estimated energy cost for beef production is higher than the 45:1 for production in the United Kingdom (Leach, 1976).

Protein production with beef cattle is especially energy-expensive because of the great cost involved in continuously maintaining the breeding herd, which has a low rate of offspring production. For each beef animal that ultimately is sent to the feedlot for fattening, an additional 1.3 breeding animals must be fed and maintained each year. Although the breeding herd is fed mainly forages, this is still a relatively costly energy system. In addition, beef cattle produce an average of 0.8 offspring per dam per year. Certainly it would be a tremendous breakthrough if beef cattle could be bred to produce an average of two per dam per year.

Beef cattle are similar to dairy cattle in that they can utilize forages for feed. Thus, it is possible to produce beef by feeding only pastures and other forages. The meat produced is considered somewhat tougher and leaner, but is often considered tastier than meat from grain-fed feedlot beef. However, more time is required to fatten the beef animal to desirable market weight when the animal is allowed to graze than when it is fattened in a feedlot.

Table 6.3 Animal protein (kg) produced per hectare in the United States (except for the last item) with various inputs of feed, labour and energy (after Pimentel *et al.*, 1975).

Animal product	Animal protein yield (kg)	Feed protein input (kg)	Feed energy input (10^3 kcal)	Fossil energy input (10^3 kcal) for the production of: Feed	Animal	Feed and animal	Labour (man-hours)	kcal ratio Feed input/protein output	Fossil energy input/protein output
Milk	59	188	6963	2382	6179	8561	23	30	35.9
Eggs	182	672	14406	6070	3490	9560	174	20	13.1
Broilers	116	651	8886	6446	3787	10233	38	19	22.1
Catfish	51	484	5007	2180	4888	7068	55	25	34.6
Pork	65	689	17021	6774	2438	9212	28	65	35.4
Beef (feedlot)	51	786	24952	7129	8716	15845	31	122	77.7
Beef (rangeland)	2.2	33	1420	0	89	89	1	164	10.1
Lamb (rangeland)	0.17	3	128	2	9	11	0.2	188	16.2
Milk, blood and Zebu cows (rangeland)	0.76	1	40	0	0	0	34	159	—

Range beef production

As mentioned, a major advantage of husbanding beef animals for
protein production is that they can be fed forage grasses and shrubs
that are unsuitable for human consumption. A typical example is
the excellent rangeland of Texas, where 2.2 kg of beef protein are
produced per hectare, compared with 50 kg produced in the feedlot
system (Table 6.2). Under more average conditions yields would be
lower, ranging from 0.2 to 0.5 kg ha^{-1} per year.

In the Texas example, an estimated 1.4×10^6 kcal of feed energy
are consumed by the range beef to produce the 2.2 kg of beef
protein. This amounts to about 164 kcal of feed energy consumed
for every kcal of beef protein produced. Although this was excellent
range, more feed energy was required (164:1) than under feedlot
conditions (122:1), because range cattle have to move about and
harvest their own feed. Under feedlot conditions, the feed is
brought to the animals. Of course, there are other differences in the
kind of feed provided for the animals, i.e. grain versus forage.

A major advantage of the rangeland over feedlot is that the fossil
energy input to produce the range beef is substantially smaller or
only about a 10 kcal input was required per kcal of range beef
protein produced compared with 78 kcal for feedlot beef. The fossil
energy input was primarily for the use of pickup trucks used in
herding the beef cattle on the range.

Lamb production

Like beef, sheep can be maintained on rangeland. Also similar to
range beef production, large land areas are needed for grazing the
sheep. Range production of lamb in Utah illustrates this.

There 0.17 kg lamb protein is produced per hectare per year from
the feed energy input of 128 000 kcal (Table 6.2). This amounts to
188 kcal of feed energy per kcal of lamb protein produced. If the
value of harvested wool were included in the analysis this ratio
would be reduced.

The fossil energy input to produce lamb protein is small, amounting to only about 16 kcal per kcal of lamb protein produced. As
with range beef production, the fossil energy input is primarily for
fuel for pickup trucks that are used for herding the sheep.

Sheep production has a slight advantage over beef cattle because
sheep, on the average, produce twins, while beef cattle usually
produce less than one calf per dam per year. Indeed, one breed of
sheep produces 5–6 offspring per gestation (J. T. Reid (1977)
personal communication). If this characteristic could be bred into
commercial breeds of sheep, the efficiency of lamb protein

production would be increased because the size of the breeding flock could be reduced. Again, it must be recognized that feeding and maintaining sufficient breeding stock necessitates a large energy expenditure.

Evaluation of Livestock Production Systems

Because of the interdependencies between kinds of plant foods consumed by animals and the availability of fossil fuel, land and labour, it is difficult to establish a simple ranking of the various livestock production systems discussed.

For example, egg and broiler production rate as the most efficient converters when only energy and land are considered. Note too, broilers are also extremely effective in use of labour.

When only forage is available then egg, broiler and pork production are eliminated and only milk, beef and lamb production are viable systems. Of these three, milk production is the most efficient converter because forage can be used and relatively small amounts of energy, land and labour are used in its production.

Turning to a comparison of beef production methods, many factors have to be weighed to determine the relative efficiencies of grain/grass-fed and grass-fed beef. For instance, beef in feedlots put on weight quickly and thus can be put on the market much sooner than those range fed. The short feeding period reduces handling period. The feedlot beef is also presently preferred by consumers because it has more fat marbling and is more tender than the grass- or range-fed animals. Balanced against these advantages must be the future outlook in availability and price of grains. If prices rise sufficiently, the grass-fed beef may have the advantage. Unfortunately, considerable energy, land and labour will have to be expended to augment production of range-fed beef (Pimentel *et al.*, 1978b). While the increased land and labour inputs are evident, the larger energy input may come as a surprise. Energy would have to be expended in the form of fertilizers and herbicides to bring marginal agricultural land into forage production.

Thus, the future outlook for animal protein is complicated and not easy to project. It is safe to say that supplies of fossil energy, availability of land and prices of grain will determine the extent and kind of production systems that will be utilized. Consumer preferences, especially in these countries where high animal protein foods are valued, may have to be modified as world populations increase and animal production is either reduced or modified.

7 Energy Use in Grain and Legume Production

Worldwide plants are extremely important sources of both calories and protein. Indeed plant foods provide over 70 % of the protein consumed by man (Pimentel *et al.*, 1975). Almost half of the plant proteins consumed by humans comes from cereal grains (Wokes, 1968; Roberts, 1976) while legumes account for about 20 % (Roberts, 1976; Pimentel *et al.*, 1975).

Recall that plant foods are also fed to livestock and then the livestock used for man's food. While some plant foods like grasses and forages are not suitable for human foods, grains and legumes most certainly are. Therefore, it is significant to note that in the United States about 50×10^6 tonnes of plant protein suitable for human consumption were diverted to livestock. Furthermore, 87 % of this was composed of nutritious cereals and legumes (Pimentel *et al.*, 1975).

Almost all or about 90 % of the plant protein/calories utilized by humans for foods is provided by fifteen major crops (Harrar, 1961; Mangelsdorf, 1966; Thurston, 1969). These crops are rice, wheat, corn (maize), sorghum, millet, rye, barley, cassava, sweet potato, potato, coconut, banana, common bean, soybean and peanut.

Of all these crops the cereal grains have always been dominant in man's food systems for several reasons. Cereals can be cultured under a wide range of environmental conditions, e.g. soil types, moisture levels and temperatures. They yield large quantities of nutrients per unit of land area. In addition, cereals have a relatively low moisture content (13–20 %) at harvest and can be transported efficiently compared with potatoes and other vegetables that are about 80 % water. This low moisture content facilitates the storage of cereal grains for long periods of time with minimal storage facilities. Finally, most cereal grains can be grown with only minor damage from pest attack.

The prime disadvantage of the protein of cereal grains is that they contain low levels of lysine, an essential amino acid (Altschul, 1958; Burton, 1965; PSAC, 1967). Also, when compared to dry legumes the dry cereal grains average about 9 % protein whereas dry legumes average about 20 % protein. Most legumes are low in the essential amino acid, methionine, but high in lysine (PSAC, 1967). Therefore, by eating combinations of cereals and legumes, man can obtain sufficient quantities of the essential amino acids to meet his daily needs. In fact, grains and legumes have long been major foods for people in those areas of the world where plant foods are the staples of the diet.

Energy Use in Grain Production

Corn (maize)

Corn is a major world cereal crop, with production totalling an estimated 334 million tonnes per year (FAO, 1977). Under favourable environmental conditions, corn is one of the most productive crops per unit area of land. For this reason, comparisons of energy input and yields will be made between producing corn by manpower, by animal power, and under full mechanization.

Manpower. In Mexico, producing corn by hand using swidden or cut/burn agricultural technology requires only a man with an axe and a hoe (Table 7.1). The total energy input for the manpower is 4120 kcal per day (Fig. 7.1). Corn production requires about 1140 hours (143 days), making the total manpower energy expended 589 160 kcal ha.$^{-1}$ When the energy for making the axe and hoe and producing the seed is added, the total energy input needed to produce corn in Mexico with only manpower is about 642 390 kcal ha.$^{-1}$ With the corn yield per hectare about 1940 kg or 6.9×10^6 kcal, the output/input ratio is about 11:1 (Table 7.1).

Table 7.1 Energy inputs in corn (maize) production in Mexico using only manpower.

	Quantity ha^{-1}	kcal ha^{-1}
Inputs		
Labour	1144 h[a]	589 160[c]
Axe and hoe	16 570 kcal[b]	16 570
Seeds	10.4 kg[b]	36 608
Total		642 338
Outputs		
Corn yield	1944 kg[a]	6 901 200
kcal output/kcal input		10.74
Protein yield	175 kg	

(a) Lewis, 1951. (b) Estimated. (c) See above.

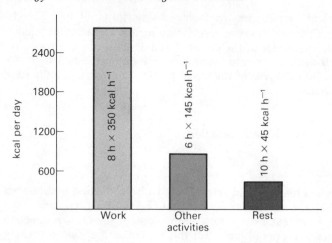

Fig. 7.1 Total energy expended per adult male in crop-raising activities employing manpower only and/or combined with animal power is calculated at 4120 kcal per day.

In this system, fossil energy is used only in the production of the axe and hoe. Based on a fossil energy input of 16 570 kcal, the output/input ratio is about 422 kcal of corn produced for each kcal of fossil fuel expended.

By comparison, producing corn in Guatemala with only manpower requires about 1420 hours per hectare, nearly 300 hours more than in Mexico (Table 7.2). Because the corn yield is only about 1070 kg ha^{-1} or about half that obtained in Mexico, the output/input ratio of 5:1 is less efficient than that of Mexico (Table 7.1).

Table 7.2 Energy inputs in corn (maize) production in Guatemala using only manpower.

	Quantity ha^{-1}	kcal ha^{-1}
Inputs		
Labour	1415 h[a]	728 725[c]
Axe and hoe	16 570 kcal[b]	16 570
Seeds	10.4 kg[b]	36 608
Total		781 903
Outputs		
Corn yield	1066 kg[a]	3 784 300
kcal output/kcal input		4.84
Protein yield	96 kg	

(a) Stadelman, 1940. (b) Estimated. (c) See page 63.

Corn produced in Nigeria requires only 620 hours labour per hectare or about half the manpower input in Mexico and Guatemala (Table 7.3). Although a small amount of fertilizer is used in Nigeria, the corn yield is still only about 1000 kg per hectare. This is less than that produced in both Mexico and Guatemala. The output/input ratio, however, is 6:1 because of the relatively low man-hour input (Table 7.3).

Table 7.3 Energy inputs in corn (maize) production in Nigeria using only manpower.

	Quantity ha^{-1}	kcal ha^{-1}
Inputs		
Labour	620 h[a]	319 300[c]
Axe and hoe	16 570 kcal[b]	16 570
Nitrogen	11 kg[a]	161 700[d]
Phosphorus	4 kg[a]	12 000[d]
Potassium	6 kg[a]	9600[d]
Seeds	10.4 kg[b]	36 608
Total		555 778
Outputs		
Corn yield	1004 kg[a]	3 564 200
kcal output/kcal input		6.41
Protein yield	90 kg	

(a) Akinwumi, 1971. (b) Estimated.
(c) See 63. (d) See Appendix A.

Although the yields of corn produced by hand are significantly less than yields of corn produced by mechanization in the United States, the reason is not the use of manpower or machine power (Fig. 7.2). The lower yields for hand-produced corn can be attributed to the reduced use of fertilizers, lack of hybrid (high yielding) varieties, poor soil and prevailing environmental conditions. Therefore, by the addition of suitable fertilizers and the use of more productive varieties of corn it should be possible to increase crop yields even when the corn producing system is manpowered.

Animal power. In Mexico, about 200 hours of ox power are needed to produce one hectare of corn. Concurrently, the man-hours needed are reduced to about 380 hours (Table 7.4). Based on the fact that producing corn by hand in Mexico requires about 1140 hours per hectare, the 200 hours of ox power reduces the manpower input by about 760 hours (Tables 7.1 and 7.4). This means that under these farming conditions 1 hour of ox power replaces nearly 4 hours of manpower.

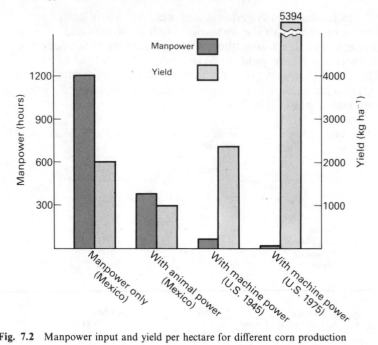

Fig. 7.2 Manpower input and yield per hectare for different corn production systems.

An ox produces 0.5–0.75 horsepower. One horsepower-hour of work, as mentioned, is equal to about 10 manpower-hours of work. Thus, 1 ox power-hour is equal to 5–7.5 manpower-hours of work. In Mexico, the 1 ox power-hour of work replaces about 4 hours of manpower (Tables 7.1 and 7.4). This is slightly lower than the theoretical 0.5–0.75 horsepower-hour capacity of ox power.

Assuming that an ox consumes about 20 000 kcal per day in feed (Pimentel, 1974), and a man consumes 4120 kcal per day, the man/ox combination requires more energy input than the man alone (Tables 7.1 and 7.4). It should be re-emphasized, however, that while man consumes mostly corn grain, the ox consumes mostly forage unsuitable for human consumption.

The total energy input for the man/ox combination is about 770 250 kcal ha^{-1}, for an output/input ratio of about 4:1. This low ratio is due to reduced corn yield, which is less than half (about 940 kg ha^{-1}) the yield obtained by manpower alone (about 1940 kg ha^{-1}) (Table 7.4). One possible reason for this is that the corn is planted on bottomland that had been in corn production for several years. In all probability this meant the fertility of the soil on this bottomland was lower than that in the slash-and-burn areas. If

Table 7.4 Energy inputs in corn (maize) production in Mexico using oxen.

	Quantity ha^{-1}	kcal ha^{-1}
Inputs		
Labour	383 h[a]	197 245[c]
Ox	198 h[a]	495 000[d]
Machinery	41 400 kcal[b]	41 400
Seeds	10.4 kg[b]	36 608
Total		770 253
Outputs		
Corn yield	941 kg	3 340 550
kcal output/kcal input		4.34
Protein yield	85 kg	

(a) Lewis, 1951. (b) Estimated. (c) See page 63. (d) Assumed 20 000 kcal of forage consumed per day by ox.

leaves and other organic matter had been added to the soil each season, the corn yields might have equalled those of the slash-and-burn technique. The man/ox hour inputs however, would increase. These inputs are needed to gather, transport and spread the organic matter.

In Guatemala, the use of about 310 hours of ox power reduces the manpower input almost in half (Table 7.5). Because the food-energy input for the man/ox combination is greater (1.2 × 10^6 kcal) than that for manpower alone (about 781 900 kcal) while the corn yields are the same, the 3:1 kcal output/kcal input is lower than for manpower alone.

Table 7.5. Energy inputs in corn (maize) production in Guatemala using an ox.

	Quantity ha^{-1}	kcal ha^{-1}
Inputs		
Labour	700 h[a]	360 500[c]
Ox	311 h[a]	777 500[d]
Machinery	41 400 kcal[b]	41 400
Seeds	10.4 kg[b]	36 608
Total		1 216 008
Outputs		
Corn yield	1066 kg[a]	3 784 300
kcal output/kcal input		3.11
Protein yield	96 kg	

(a) Stadelman, 1940. (b) Estimated. (c) See 63. (d) Assumed 20 000 kcal of forage consumed per day by ox.

When using carabao draft animals in the Philippines, the man and animal inputs are similar to the inputs used in Mexico when man and animal power are combined (Table 7.6). The corn yield is also similar even though some fertilizer was used in the Philippines. It is somewhat surprising to find such close similarity in both inputs and corn yields in two systems located in different parts of the world where cultures also differ.

Table 7.6　Energy inputs in corn (maize) production in Philippines.

	Quantity ha^{-1}	kcal ha^{-1}
Inputs		
Labour	296 h[a]	152 440[c]
Carabao	182 h[a]	364 325[d]
Machinery	41 400 kcal[b]	41 400
Nitrogen	4 kg[a]	58 800[e]
Phosphorus	1 kg[a]	3 000[e]
Potassium	0.3 kg[a]	480[e]
Seeds	10.4 kg[b]	36 608
Transportation	3 000 kcal	3 000 kcal
Total		660 053
Outputs		
Corn yield	941 kg	3 340 550
kcal output/kcal input		5.06
Protein yield	85 kg	

(a) AED, 1960; FAO, 1961; Allan, 1961. (b) Estimated. (c) See page 63. (d) Assumed 20 000 kcal of forage consumed per day by ox. (e) Appendix A.

Machine power.　The energetics of mechanized agriculture are distinctly different from those of labour-intensive agriculture. Corn production in the United States is a typical example of heavy reliance on machines for power. First, as expected, the total man-power input is dramatically reduced compared to the systems previously discussed. In fact, it averages only 12 hours per hectare (Table 7.7). The total energy input per day in manpower is calculated to be 3720 kcal (Fig. 7.3). Therefore, 12 hours of labour represents a total energy input of 5580 kcal, or substantially less than that expended in any of the other agricultural systems previously discussed.

Balanced against this low manpower input is the significant increase in fossil energy input needed to run the machines that replace man. Thus in the United States in 1975 the fossil fuel energy inputs average about 7.0×10^6 kcal ha^{-1} of corn or the equivalent of about 700 litres of gasoline. The corn yield is high, about 5390 kg ha^{-1}, or the equivalent of 19.1×10^6 kcal energy, for an output/input ratio of about 3:1.

Table 7.7 Energy inputs per hectare in U.S. corn production in 1975.

	Quantity ha^{-1}	kcal ha^{-1}
Inputs		
Labour	12 h[a]	5580
Machinery	31 kg[b]	558 000[b]
Diesel	112 litres[c]	1 278 368[c]
Nitrogen	128 kg[d]	1 881 600[d]
Phosphorus	72 kg[d]	216 000[d]
Potassium	80 kg[d]	128 000[d]
Limestone	100 kg[e]	31 500[e]
Seeds	21 kg[f]	525 000[f]
Irrigation	780 000 kcal[g]	780 000
Insecticides	1 kg[h]	86 910[h]
Herbicides	2 kg[h]	199 820[h]
Drying	426 341 kcal[i]	426 341[i]
Electricity	380 000 kcal[j]	380 000
Transportation	136 kg[k]	34 952
Total		6 532 071
Outputs		
Corn yield	5394 kg[l]	19 148 700
kcal output/kcal input		2.93
Protein yield	485 kg	

(a) Estimated. (b) An estimated 31.40 tonnes of machinery is used to manage about 100 ha and it is assumed that the machinery depreciates over 10 years. (c) Fuel includes that used in tractors, combines, trucks and automobiles. Most of this fuel was assumed to be diesel fuel. See Appendix B. (d) Average fertilizer use in corn production (USDA, 1974a). (e) Lime use estimated based on FEDS data (USDA, 1977b). (f) Seeds estimated based on planting density of 62 000 plants per hectare. Energy value for hybrid seed is estimated at 25 000 kcal kg^{-1} (Heichel, 1978). (g) An estimated 3.8 % of the corn grain is irrigated in the U.S. Water was assumed to be pumped from a 30 m depth and sprinkler irrigated (Batty and Keller, 1978). (h) Application rates of insecticides and herbicides from USDA, 1974b. The energy values calculated from data in Appendix C. (i) An estimated 40 % of the corn is dried and the assumption was the corn was field harvested with 26 % moisture and dried to 13 %. For each kg of water removed, the energy expenditure was 1520 kcal (Pimentel *et al.*, 1973). (j) Electrical use was assumed to be 380 000 kcal per hectare. (k) A total of 136 kg of goods were transported to the farm. It was assumed that the average distance that the goods were transported was 640 km. The energy cost to transport a kg of material was 257 kcal (see Chapter 11). (l) USDA, 1976a.

Obviously output/input ratios are influenced by both crop yields and energy inputs. This is clearly illustrated by a comparison of data for U.S. corn production in 1945 and 1975. Since 1945 the total energy inputs have increased about three-fold and this has resulted in a decline in the output/input ratio from 3.7 to 2.9, or about a 22 % decline (Pimentel *et al.*, 1973). During this period

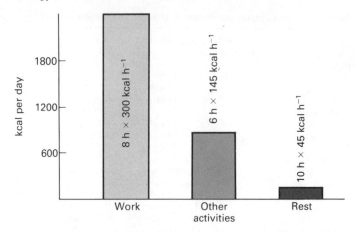

Fig. 7.3 Total energy expended per adult male in crop-raising activities employing machinery is calculated at 3720 kcal per day.

fossil fuel has been relatively cheap so the decline in energy ratios has not reduced the economic benefits received from the greater corn yields.

The fossil energy inputs into U.S. corn production are primarily from petroleum and natural gas. Nitrogen fertilizer, which requires natural gas for production, represents the largest single input, or more than 27 % of the total fossil energy inputs (Table 7.7). Machinery and fuel together total about 28 % of the fossil energy input. Taken as a whole, about half of the energy inputs in U.S. corn production reduce man and animal labour inputs, and about half increase corn productivity.

The energy inputs for corn production and corn yield in the United States are similar to those reported by Leach (1976) for the United Kingdom (Table 7.8). Less fertilizer is used in the United Kingdom than in the United States, but more fossil energy is used for corn drying in the United Kingdom than in the United States. However, the overall output/input ratios of 2:1 are in general agreement. Note that no labour input was used in the calculations for the United Kingdom.

Wheat

Wheat is the single most important cereal crop in the world today and more humans eat wheat than any other cereal grain. The total annual yield of about 420×10^6 tonnes (FAO, 1977) is achieved in diverse production systems, ranging from man/animal power to almost complete reliance on machines. As with corn production,

Table 7.8 Energy inputs in maize (corn) production in the United Kingdom (after Leach, 1976).

	Quantity ha^{-1}	GJ ha^{-1}
Inputs		
Tractors	17.3 h ×189 MJ h^{-1}	3.27
Combine	2.5 h (est. 220 MJ h^{-1})	0.55
Other machinery	£28.4 (×est. 100 MJ £$^{-1}$)	2.84
Nitrogen	56 kg	4.48
Phosphorus	45 kg	0.63
Potassium	45 kg	0.40
Sprays	£7.4 est. as cereals	0.40
Drying, fuel	270 litre	11.67
Drying, electricity	148 kWh	2.13
Total		26.37
Outputs		
Maize yield	5020 kg	61.7
kcal output/kcal input		2.34
Protein yield	452 kg	

4186 J = 1 kcal.

both energy inputs and yields vary with each system and therefore influence ultimate output/input ratios.

For example, producing wheat in the Uttar Pradesh region of India illustrates the use of man/bullock power (Table 7.9). There a total energy input of about 2.8 ×10^6 kcal is required to attain a wheat yield of 2.7 ×10^6 kcal of food energy. As a result, the output/input ratio is 0.96:1, or less wheat energy produced than energy expended, or no net gain in wheat energy over energy used in production.

This negative output/input ratio may be somewhat misleading, because one of the large inputs of this production system (2.2 ×10^6 kcal) is for the two bullocks (Table 7.9). Because the bullocks consume primarily grasses and little or no grain, they are in fact a type of food conversion system. The bullocks convert the grass energy into wheat energy through their labour in the wheat fields. If the bullock input were removed from the analysis, then the input/output ratio would be more favourable and would increase to 5 kcal per kcal input, which is a more realistic representation of what occurs.

The only fossil energy input in this man/bullock system is that expended for machinery. If the output/input ratio is based only on the fossil energy input, it is an efficient 65:1 (Table 7.9).

In contrast with the relatively simple Indian production system, wheat production in the United States has many more energy inputs (Table 7.10). Large machinery powered by fossil energy replaces animal power and drastically cuts manpower. The machinery and

Table 7.9   Energy inputs in wheat production using bullocks in Uttar Pradesh, India.

	Quantity ha^{-1}	kcal ha^{-1}
Inputs		
Labour	615 h[a]	324 413[c]
Bullock (pair)	321 h (each)[a]	2 247 500[d]
Machinery	41 400 kcal[b]	41 400
Manure	(included in labour and bullock)	
Irrigation	(included in labour and bullock)	
Seeds	65 kg[b]	214 500
Total		2 827 813
Outputs		
Wheat Yield	821 kg[a]	2 709 300
kcal output/kcal input		0.96
Protein yield	99 kg	

(a) MFACDCGI, 1966. (b) Estimated. (c) See page 63. (d) Assumed each bullock consumed 20 000 kcal of forage per day.

Table 7.10.   Energy inputs in U.S. wheat production.

	Quantity ha^{-1}	kcal ha^{-1}
Inputs		
Labour	7 h[a]	3255
Machinery	20 kg[b]	360 000
Diesel	53 litres[c]	604 942[e]
Nitrogen	50 kg[a]	715 000[f]
Phosphorus	26 kg[a]	78 000[f]
Potassium	30 kg[a]	48 000[f]
Limestone	35 kg[d]	11 025[f]
Seeds	106 kg[a]	699 600
Herbicides	0.5 kg[a]	49 955[g]
Electricity	200 000 kcal[h]	200 000
Transportation	177 kg[i]	45 489[i]
Total		2 815 266
Output		
Wheat yield	2 060 kg[j]	6 798 000
kcal output/kcal input		2.41
Protein yield	247 kg	

(a) Kearl, 1962; Mullins and Grant, 1968. (b) Estimated. (c) Estimated based on FEDS data (USDA, 1977b). (d) Estimated. (e) Appendix B. (f) Appendix A. (g) Appendix C. (h) Estimated. (i) 177 kg ×257 kcal kg^{-1}.(j) Average wheat yield in United States (USDA, 1976a).

use of fertilizers, while increasing wheat yield per hectare, also significantly increase the use of fossil fuel energy over that expended in the man/bullock system. A 2:1 ratio results from the 2.8×10^6 kcal energy inputs used to produce 6.8×10^6 kcal wheat energy.

Energy inputs for wheat production in the United Kingdom are listed in Table 7.11. Fertilizer inputs and wheat yields are both greater in the United Kingdom than in the United States. As a result of the substantially higher yields, the 4:1 output/input ratio for the United Kingdom is nearly double that of 2:1 for the United States. Although energy inputs for manpower were not included in the U.K. analysis, this input is relatively small for all highly mechanized systems, and therefore the ratio would not have been changed significantly with its inclusion.

Table 7.11 Energy inputs in winter wheat production in the U.K. (after Leach, 1976).

	Quantity/ha	GJ/ha
Inputs		
Field work, tractors	3.24 GJ	3.24
Field work, equipment	1.29 GJ	1.29
Nitrogen	95 kg	
Phosphorus	55 kg 8.87	8.87
Potassium	55 kg	
Sprays, 4 kg	4 kg	0.40
Drying, fuels (390 MJ/t)	1.67 GJ	1.67
Drying, machinery (130 MJ/t)	0.56 GJ	0.56
Total		16.03
Outputs		
Wheat yield	3780 kg	56.2
kcal output/kcal input		3.51
Protein yield	452 kg	

4186 J = 1 kcal.

Oats

In the United States, oats are a highly productive grain crop (Table 7.12). In an average year 2.1×10^6 kcal ha^{-1} energy input yields 6.7×10^6 kcal of food energy. The output/input ratio, therefore, is 3:1, or higher than that for wheat.

As with U.S. wheat production, the manpower per hectare input is relatively small while the fossil energy input used to run the machines is one of the major energy inputs.

For comparison, the energy inputs for oats and barley production in the United Kingdom are listed in Table 7.13. Note that in the United Kingdom greater amounts of fertilizer are used and the crop yields are correspondingly greater than in the United States. The output/input ratios, however, are similar.

Table 7.12. Energy inputs in U.S. oat production.

	Quantity ha^{-1}	kcal ha^{-1}
Input		
Labour	6 h[a]	2790
Machinery	20 kg[b]	360 000[b]
Diesel	45 litres[c]	513 630
Nitrogen	15 kg[a]	220 500[e]
Phosphorus	12 kg[a]	36 000[e]
Potassium	21 kg[a]	33 600[e]
Limestone	30 kg[c]	9450[e]
Seeds	93 kg[a]	725 400[f]
Herbicides	0.2 kg[a]	19 982[g]
Electricity	200 000 kcal[h]	200 000
Transportation	158 kg	40 606[i]
Total		2 161 958
Outputs		
Oat yield	1732[d]	6 719 700
kcal output/kcal input		3.11
Protein yield	242 kg	

(a) USDA, 1971b. (b) Estimated. (c) Estimated and energy input based on Appendix B. (d) Average U.S. oat yields (USDA, 1976a). (e) Appendix A. (f) Energy content of seeds was doubled. (g) Appendix C. (h) Estimated based on FEDS data (USDA, 1977b). (i) 158 kg ×257 kcal kg^{-1}

Table 7.13 Energy inputs in oat and barley production in the United Kingdom (after Leach, 1976).

	Quantity ha^{-1}	GJ ha^{-1}
Inputs		
Nitrogen	97 kg	7.76
Phosphorus	48 kg	0.67
Potassium	48 kg	0.43
Field work, tractors	3.24 GJ	3.24
Field work, equipment	1.29 GJ	1.29
Sprays	4 kg	0.40
Drying, fuels	390 MJ/t	1.40
Drying, machinery	130 MJ/t	0.47
Total		15.66
Outputs		
Oats/barley yield	3410 kg	37.2
kcal output/kcal input		2.4
Protein yield	477 kg	

4186 J = 1 kcal.

Rice

A total of 345 ×10^6 tonnes of rice are produced annually in the world (FAO, 1966). Indeed, rice is the staple food for an estimated

2000 million humans, mostly those living in the developing countries (FAO, 1966). This makes an analysis of various techniques used in rice production particularly relevant.

Rice production by the Iban tribe of Borneo is a typical example of manpower production (Table 7.14). Freeman (1955) reported that a total of 1186 man hours of labour is required per hectare (Table 7.14). In this swidden rice production, both virgin and secondary forest growth is cut and burned for subsequent rice culture. Energy inputs for a hectare of rice total 1.0×10^6 kcal, with about 2/3 rds of this expended for manpower labour and the other 1/3 rd for seeds. The yield is about 2020 kg ha^{-1} or about 7.3×10^6 kcal food energy. Thus, the output/input ratio is 7:1, denoting a relatively high return for the investment.

Table 7.14 Energy inputs in rice production for the Iban of Borneo using only manpower (Freeman, 1955).

	Quantity ha^{-1}	kcal ha^{-1}
Inputs		
Labour	1186 h[a]	625 615
Axe and hoe	16 570 kcal[b]	16 570
Seeds	108 kg[a]	392 040[c]
Total		1 034 225
Outputs		
Rice yield	2016 kg[a]	7 318 080
kcal output/kcal input		7.08
Protein yield	141 kg	

(a) Freeman, 1955. (b) Estimated for construction of axe and hoe.
(c) Estimated and direct food energy content of rice used in planting.

Again, with the exception of Japan, there appears to be an association between manpower input and yield, that is, as manpower increases, yields decline (Figure 7.4). As with corn, equally high yields of rice can be grown employing only manpower when appropriate high yielding rice varieties, fertilizers, and other technologies are also used.

In the Philippines, both man and animal power are used in rice production (Table 7.15). Total energy inputs are 1.8×10^6 kcal to produce about 1650 kg of rice, which has the equivalent of 6.0×10^6 kcal food energy. The resulting output/input ratio is 3:1, about half that of the Iban rice production. As with the use of bullock for wheat production in the Philippines, the carabao convert grass energy into rice energy. If energy input of carabao is removed from the accounting, since this is renewable energy, then the output/input ratio rises to 10:1.

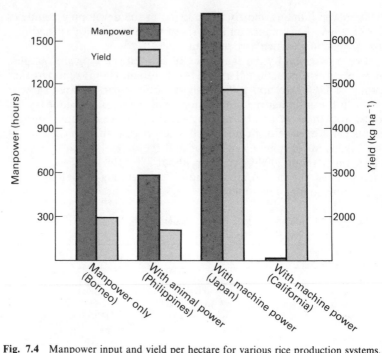

Fig. 7.4 Manpower input and yield per hectare for various rice production systems.

Table 7.15 Energy inputs and return in rice production in the Philippines, using carabao (after Pimentel, 1976). Energetic cost of irrigation was included in labour and carabao.

	Quantity ha^{-1}	kcal ha^{-1}
Inputs		
Labour	576 h[a]	303 840[b]
Equipment	41 424 kg[c]	41 424[c]
Carabao	272 h[a]	952 000[d]
Nitrogen	5.6 kg[a]	85 008[e]
Seeds	108 kg[a]	399 600[f]
Herbicide	0.6 kg[a]	43 560[g]
Total		1 825 432 kcal
Outputs		
Rice yield	1654 kg[a]	6 004 020[h]
kcal output/kcal input		3.29
Protein yield	116 kg	

(a) De Los Reyes *et al.*, 1965. (b) See page 63. (c) Estimated for machinery. (d) Inputs for carabao were assumed to be similar to oxen, see page 66. (e) Appendix A. (f) De Los Reyes *et al.*, 1965, valued rice seed at 3700 kcal kg^{-1}. (g) Appendix C. (h) White rice contains 3630 kcal kg^{-1}.

As with other grains, rice production in the United States uses large inputs of energy, particularly fossil fuel energy (Table 7.16). Based on data from rice production in California, the average yield of 6160 kg ha^{-1} (22.4 $\times 10^6$ kcal) is significantly greater than in the other systems discussed. However, the high energy input of 14.4 $\times 10^6$ kcal results in the low 1.6:1 output/input ratio. While major energy inputs are for machinery and fuel, fertilizers account for about 37 % of the total fossil fuel input. The other inputs are for irrigation, seeds and drying. Although the manpower dropped to 17 hours per hectare, it is relatively high for grain production in the United States.

Table 7.16 Energy inputs in California rice production.

	Quantity ha^{-1}	kcal ha^{-1}
Inputs		
Labour	17 h[a]	7905[b]
Machinery	20 kg[c]	360 000[c]
Diesel	286 litres[d]	3 264 404[e]
Gasoline	65 litres[d]	657 085[e]
Liquid petroleum gas	46 litres[d]	354 430[e]
Nitrogen	280 kg[f]	4 116 000[h]
Phosphorus	67 kg[f]	201 000[h]
Limestone	35 kg[g]	11 025[h]
Seeds	157 kg[a]	1 139 820[i]
Irrigation (natural gas)	110 m^3[d]	1 299 430[d]
Insecticides	2.2 kg[a]	191 202[j]
Herbicides	11.2 kg[a]	1 118 992[j]
Drying	6160 kg[a]	1 217 216[k]
Electricity	380 000 kcal[g]	380 000[g]
Transportation	471 kg	121 047[l]
Total		14 439 556
Outputs		
Rice yield	6160 kg[a]	22 360 800
kcal output/kcal input		1.55
Protein yield	462 kg	

(a) Grant, Amarel and Johnson, 1971. (b) See page 63. (c) Estimated. (d) FEA, 1976a. (e) Appendix B. (f) Cervinka *et al.*, 1974. (g) Estimated. (h) Appendix A. (i) Energy content of seed doubled. (j) Appendix C. (k) Crop dried from 26 % to 13 % moisture at 1520 kcal kg^{-1} water removed. (l) 471 kg $\times$257 kcal kg^{-1}

By comparison, rice production in Japan is still relatively labour-intensive, requiring about 1730 hours of manpower per hectare (Table 7.17). Although in Japan the rice yields are lower, the fossil energy inputs also are lower than in the United States. This results in an output/input ratio of 2.5:1 for Japanese-produced rice, com-

Table 7.17   Energy inputs in rice production in Japan.

	Quantity ha^{-1}	kcal ha^{-1}
Inputs		
Labour	1729 h[a]	803 985
Machinery	10 kg[b]	180 000[b]
Gasoline	90 litres[c]	909 810[c]
Nitrogen	142 kg[d]	2 087 400[d]
Phosphorus	75 kg[d]	225 000[d]
Potassium	88 kg[a]	140 800[d]
Seeds	112 kg[e]	813 120[e]
Irrigation	90 litres[f]	909 810[f]
Insecticides	4 kg[g]	347 640[g]
Herbicides	7 kg[g]	699 370[g]
Electricity	2.6 kWh[h]	7400[h]
Transportation	200 kg[i]	51 400
Total		7 175 735
Outputs		
Rice yields	4 848 kg[j]	17 598 240
kcal output/kcal input		2.45
Protein yield	364 kg	

(a) Matsubayashi *et al.*, 1963. (b) Estimated. (c) Estimated based on intensive management and small size of tractors (see Appendix B). (d) Allan, 1961; and Appendix A. (e) Estimated from Grant and Mullins, 1963, and energy content of seeds doubled. (f) Estimated based on U.S. power requirements. (g) Estimate based on FAO, 1963, statistics on pesticides used in Japan (see Appendix C). (h) Estimated (see Appendix B). (i) 200 kg ×257 kcal kg^{-1}. (j) Rice yield for 1960–64 for Japan (USDA, 1971a).

pared to 1.6:1 for U.S.-produced rice, and reflects a more efficient production system in Japan.

Sorghum

Sorghum is used extensively in Africa for food. The available data on sorghum production in the Sudan indicates that the production of sorghum by hand requires less manpower than producing corn in Mexico by hand (Tables 7.1 and 7.18). In the Sudan, only 240 hours per hectare (Table 7.18) are required for sorghum production, compared with about 1140 hours per hectare for corn in Mexico (Table 7.1). Manpower is the major energy input, costing more than half the total energy input. The hoe is the only fossil energy input in the system and costs only about 16570 kcal (Table 7.18). When the yield of 900 kg ha^{-1} is converted into 3.0 ×10^6 kcal food energy, the resulting output/input ratio is 14:1. This is a relatively high production ratio.

Table 7.18 Energy inputs in sorghum production in the Sudan using primarily manpower.

	Quantity ha^{-1}	kcal ha^{-1}
Inputs		
Labour	240 h[a]	126 600[d]
Hoe	16 570 kcal[b]	16 570
Seeds	19 kg[c]	62 700
Total		205 870
Outputs		
Sorghum yield	900 kg[a]	2 970 000
kcal output/kcal input		14.43
Protein yield	108 kg	

(a) BDPA, 1965. (b) Estimated. (c) Estimated. (d) See page 63.

Sorghum production in the United States uses large inputs of energy, mainly fossil energy for making and running machines and for producing fertilizer (Table 7.19). Thus, although the 3030 kg ha^{-1} yield is over three times greater than that of the Sudan, the final output/input ratio of 2:1 is significantly lower than that of the Sudan.

A comparison of sorghum and corn production in the United States shows that the inputs are quite similar (Tables 7.7 and 7.19). The yields for sorghum, however, are about 3030 kg ha^{-1}, or considerably lower than the average corn yield of about 5390 kg ha^{-1}. One reason for the lower sorghum yield is that sorghum is produced mainly in dry regions, while corn is grown in areas that have climatic conditions more suitable for growing crops.

Energy Use in Legume Production

Peas, beans and lentils, all members of the Leguminosae family, are extremely important plant foods, especially in those areas of the world where animal foods are scarce and expensive or where religious or cultural reasons dictate the avoidance of animal flesh as food. Most legumes have a high carbohydrate content of 55–60 % and also a high protein content of 20–30 %. The 40–45 % protein content of soybeans is exceptionally high for plants. In addition to protein, legumes are excellent plant sources of iron and thiamine.

Soybeans

Because of its high protein content, the soybean is probably the single most important protein crop in the world. An estimated

Table 7.19.   Energy inputs per hectare in U.S. sorghum production.

	Quantity ha[-1]	kcal ha[-1]
Inputs		
Labour	12 h[a]	5 580
Machinery	31 kg[b]	558 000[b]
Diesel	135 litres[a]	1 540 890[g]
Nitrogen	78 kg[c]	1 146 600[h]
Phosphorus	31 kg[c]	93 000[h]
Potassium	10 kg[c]	16 000[h]
Limestone	30 kg[a]	9 450[h]
Seeds	30 kg[a]	420 000[i]
Irrigation	625 000 kcal[d]	625 000
Insecticides	1 kg[e]	86 910[j]
Herbicides	4.5 kg[e]	449 595[j]
Electricity	380 000 kcal[f]	380 000
Transportation	162 kg	41 634[k]
Total		5 372 659
Outputs		
Sorghum yield	3 031 kg[e]	10 547 880
kcal output/kcal input		1.96
Protein yield	344 kg	

(a) Estimated. (b) An estimated 31.40 tonnes of machinery is used to manage about 100 ha, and it is assumed that the machinery depreciates over 10 years. (c) USDA, 1974a. (d) An estimated 4% of sorghum was irrigated. (e) Based on USDA, 1975a. (f) Electrical use was assumed to be 380 000 kcal ha[-1]. (g) Based on Appendix B. (h) Based on Appendix A. (i) Heichel, 1978. (j) Based on Appendix C. (k) 162 kg × 257 kcal kg[-1].

62.1 × 10[6] tonnes were produced worldwide in 1976 (FAO, 1977). About 75% of all soybeans produced are grown in the United States, with China the second largest producer (FAO, 1977). In the United States, relatively little of the soy crop is used as human food. Instead, the bean is processed for its valuable oil and the seed cake and soybean meal are fed to livestock. Soybeans and soy products head the list of U.S. agricultural exports (USDA, 1976a) and therefore are an important factor in the U.S. balance of export/import payments.

In the United States, soybean yields an average in food energy amounting to 7.6 × 10[6] kcal ha[-1] (Table 7.20). With inputs for production of 1.8 × 10[6] kcal ha[-1], the output/input ratio is 4:1. The two largest inputs are for herbicides and seeding the soybeans; the third largest input is for manufacturing the machinery. Note that the yield of protein is high, and also greater than any other legume tabulated (Table 7.20).

All legume production is unique in that the necessary nitrogen input is substantially less than that for most other crops. For exam-

Table 7.20 Energy inputs in U.S. soybean production

	Quantity ha^{-1}	kcal ha^{-1}
Inputs		
Labour	10 h[a]	4650
Machinery	20 kg[b]	360 000[b]
Diesel	7 litres[a]	79 898[d]
Gasoline	5 litres[a]	50 545[d]
Nitrogen	4 kg[a]	58 800[e]
Phosphorus	18 kg[a]	54 000[e]
Potassium	47 kg[a]	75 200[e]
Lime	350 kg[a]	110 250[e]
Seeds	60 kg[a]	480 000[f]
Herbicides	5 kg[a]	499 550[g]
Electricity	10 kWh[a]	28 630[h]
Transportation	100 kg	25 700[i]
Total		1 827 223
Outputs		
Soybean yield	1882 kg[c]	7 584 460
kcal output/kcal input		4.15
Protein yield	640 kg	

(a) FEDS data (USDA, 1977b). (b) Estimated. (c) USDA, 1976a.
(d) Appendix B. (e) Appendix A. (f) Heichel, 1978. (g) Appendix C.
(h) Appendix B. (i) 100 kg ×257 kcal kg^{-1}.

ple, soybeans require only 1/10th that needed for corn production
(Tables 7.7 and 7.20). This is because soybeans and other legumes
can obtain nitrogen from the atmosphere through their symbiotic
relationship with microorganisms in the soil. The nitrogen fixation
process carried on by the microorganisms uses up about 5 % of
the light energy captured by the soybean plants. In other words, if
all the light energy captured by the plant were put only into bean
production and none used for nitrogen fixation then it would be
possible to produce more soybeans. Nitrogen fixation saves on fertilizer. Thus, to supply 100 kg of commercial fertilizer to replace the
nitrogen fixed by legumes would necessitate the expenditure of
1 520 000 kcal of fossil energy.

Obviously it is more economical for plants to meet their own
nitrogen needs rather than for man to make and apply fertilizer.
The 100 kg of soybean yield that is lost because of the energy
directed to nitrogen fixation amounts to about $25 ($6 bu^{-1}) and is
much less than the $48 cost of the 100 kg ha^{-1} nitrogen produced
by the plants.

Dry beans

The energy inputs for producing dry beans are quite similar to those for soybeans (Table 7.21). Average dry bean yields of 1460 kg ha^{-1} are lower, however, than the 1880 kg ha^{-1} for soybeans, resulting in an output/input ratio of only 1.8:1 for dry beans. In addition, the protein yield is about half that of soybeans.

Table 7.21   Energy inputs in U.S. dry bean production.

	Quantity ha^{-1}	kcal ha^{-1}
Inputs		
Labour	10 h[a]	4650
Machinery	20 kg[b]	360 000[b]
Diesel	76 litres[c]	867 464[g]
Nitrogen	16 kg[d]	235 200[h]
Phosphorus	18 kg[d]	54 000[h]
Potassium	47 kg[d]	75 200[h]
Lime	350 kg[a]	110 250[h]
Seeds	60 kg[a]	480 000[a]
Insecticides	1 kg[e]	86 910[i]
Herbicides	4 kg[e]	399 640[i]
Electricity	10 kWh[f]	28 630[f]
Transportation	148 kg	38 036[j]
Total		2 739 980
Outputs		
Dry bean yield	1457 kg[k]	4 953 800
kcal output/kcal input		1.81
Protein yield	325 kg	

(a) Estimated from soybean data. (b) Estimated. (c) Estimated. (d) Assumed to be similar to U.S. soybean production. See Table 7.20. (e) Estimated. (f) Estimated from soybean data and Appendix B. (g) Appendix B. (h) Appendix A. (i) Appendix C. (j) 148 kg ×257 kcal kg^{-1}. (k) USDA, 1976a.

Cowpeas

Cowpeas are also a major legume crop in many parts of the world (FAO, 1977). Energy input data on the production of cowpeas in north central Nigeria illustrate a manpower system (Doering, 1977). The total energy input is 811 800 kcal, while the yield for this region is 5.2 ×10^6 kcal with a labour input of 814 hours (Table 7.22). This results in an output/input ratio of 6.5:1 for this particular cowpea production system.

Peanuts

Annually an estimated 18.5 ×10^6 tonnes of peanuts or groundnuts

Table 7.22 Energy inputs in north central Nigeria cowpea production.

	Quantity ha^{-1}	kcal ha^{-1}
Inputs		
Labour	814 h[a]	419 210[c]
Hoe and other equipment	16 570[b]	16 570[b]
Insecticides	5.6 litres[b]	319 100[a]
Seeds	16.8 kg[a]	57 000[a]
Total		811 880
Outputs		
Cowpea yield	1 530 kg[a]	5 247 900[a]
kcal output/kcal input		6.46
Protein yield	428 kg[a]	

(a) Doering, 1977. (b) Estimated. (c) See page 63.

are produced in the world (FAO, 1977). In addition to the direct use of peanuts for food, they are grown for their valuable oil.

Data on the production of peanuts employing a large input of labour (936 hours) for northeast Thailand has been reported by Doering (1977) (Table 7.23). The inputs, including the large labour input total 1.9×10^6 kcal and the yield is 5.0×10^6 kcal. Thus the output/input ratio for this peanut production system is 2.6:1 (Table 7.23).

Table 7.23 Energy inputs in northeast Thailand peanut (groundnut) production.

	Quantity ha^{-1}	kcal ha^{-1}
Inputs		
Labour	936 h[a]	585 040[b]
Draft buffalo	0.17 buffalo[a]	1 116 000[a]
Equipment	16 570 kcal[d]	16 570[d]
Insecticides	108 700 kcal[a]	108 700[a]
Nitrogen	2 kg[a]	29 400[c]
Phosphorus	2 kg[a]	6 000[c]
Potassium	2 kg[a]	3 200[c]
Seeds	15 kg (unshelled)[a]	58 500[a]
Total		1 923 410
Outputs		
Peanut yield	1 280 kg[a]	4 992 000[a]
kcal output/kcal input		2.60
Protein yield	218 kg[a]	

(a) Doering, 1977. (b) See page 63. (c) Appendix A. (d) Estimated.

Peanut production in the United States (Georgia) yields 15.3×10^6 kcal or about three times that in Thailand. However, with the large number of inputs the output/input ratio is only 1.4:1 (Table 7.24).

Table 7.24   Energy inputs in peanuts (groundnuts) produced in Georgia, USA (Pimentel *et al.*, 1978a).

	Quantity ha^{-1}	kcal ha^{-1}
Inputs		
Labour	19 h	8835
Machinery	20 kg	360 000
Gasoline	63 litres	636 867
Diesel	125 litres	1 426 750
Electricity	40 997 kcal	40 997
Nitrogen	33 kg	485 100
Phosphorus	69 kg	207 000
Potassium	112 kg	179 200
Lime	1362 kg	408 600
Seeds	127 kg	2 286 000
Insecticides	37 kg	3 215 670
Herbicides	16 kg	1 598 560
Transportation	335 kg	86 095
Total		10 947 674
Output		
Peanut yield	3 724 kg	15 305 640
kcal output/kcal input		1.4
Protein yield	320 kg	

Of importance in the future will be to find viable ways to increase yields of grains and legumes per hectare while keeping the output/input ratios efficient.

Yields can be increased by developing through plant breeding improved varieties of grains and legumes that have high yield characteristics. IR-8 rice, developed at the International Rice Research Institute, is one illustration of high yield grain crop. Yields can also be augmented by the judicious use of fertilizers. Newer varieties of plants should be resistant to the naturally occurring pests that all too often reduce yields and also make necessary more pesticide treatment. Both fertilizers and pesticides cost in fossil fuel energy and this is part of the efficiency ratio.

Obviously all parts of the production system that depend on fossil energy will be constrained as supplies of this non-renewable resource decrease and prices increase.

A greater problem facing us in the future will be to what extent we choose to consume plant proteins directly and whether we can afford to cycle large quantities through animals. The production of animal protein costs not only in terms of energy, labour and land needed to grow the plants but also the direct cost of animal husbandry itself. Then, too, the relatively inefficient conversion of plant protein into animal protein makes it clear that animal protein is expensive to produce by whatever criteria we set.

8 Energy Use in Fruit, Vegetable and Forage Production

Fruits

Fruits, the edible material adhering to the seeds of a plant, are eaten either raw, cooked or dried. Fruits have a high water content, ranging from about 75 to 90%. Carbohydrate, usually in the form of sugar, is the second largest constituent, ranging from about 6 to 22%. Fruits contain only small amounts of protein and negligible amounts of fats. Citrus fruits, cantaloupes and strawberries are excellent sources of vitamin C, while yellow-orange fruits are considered good sources of carotene, the precursor of vitamin A.

Apple and orange production in the United States are analyzed as examples of energy expenditure and food energy yield in fruit.

Apples

Apples are an economically valuable crop. An estimated 3.2×10^6 tonnes of apples are produced annually in the United States and are valued $538 million (USDA, 1975a). Petroleum used to operate the many types of machinery employed in apple orchards accounts for about 50% of the total energy input (Table 8.1). The next largest input is for pesticides, which represent about 26% of the total energy input.

The labour input of 175 hours per hectare expended in apple production is high compared with most other food crops grown in the United States. Most of this manpower input occurs during the harvesting of the fruit. The total energy input for labour is calculated to be about 81 380 kcal ha^{-1} and is only 0.5% of the total energy input for apple production, which is 18.3×10^6 kcal. The yield in fruit is about 9.6×10^6 kcal ha^{-1}. Thus the output/input ratio is only 0.5:1 or roughly 2 kcal of energy are necessary to produce each kcal of apple.

Oranges

Oranges are another valuable fruit and annually, in the United

Table 8.1 Energy inputs in U.S. apple production.

	Quantity ha^{-1}	kcal ha^{-1}
Inputs		
Labour	175 h[b]	81 375[c]
Machinery	35 kg[b]	630 000
Diesel	560 litres[a]	6 391 840[d]
Gasoline	245 litres[a]	2 476 705[d]
Nitrogen	190 kg[a]	2 793 000[e]
Potassium	41 kg[a]	65 600[e]
Limestone	45 kg[b]	14 175[e]
Irrigation	320 000 kcal[a]	320 000
Insecticides	30 kg[a]	2 607 300[f]
Herbicides	2 kg[a]	199 820[f]
Fungicides	30 kg[a]	1 947 300[f]
Electricity	310 000 kcal[b]	310 000[b]
Transportation	635 kg	163 195[g]
Total		18 000 310
Outputs		
Apple yield	17 920 kg[a]	9 587 200
kcal output/kcal input		0.53
Protein yield	36 kg	

(a) FEA, 1976a. (b) Estimated. (c) 175 h ×465 kcal h^{-1}. (d) See Appendix B.
(e) See Appendix A. (f) See Appendix C. (g) 635 kg ×257 kcal kg^{-1}.

States, 9.3×10^6 tonnes are produced. Although oranges and other citrus fruits have more than double the vitamin C content of potatoes, about half as much vitamin C in the U.S. diet is obtained from potatoes as from citrus fruits (USDA, 1975b).

In production technology and energy inputs, oranges do not differ significantly from apples (Table 8.1). Orange production uses slightly more petroleum than apple production but only half as much pesticide. The return in food energy in the form of oranges is 6.8×10^6 kcal, for an output/input ratio of only 0.4:1. Thus nearly 3 kcal of energy are required to produce one kcal of orange. Based on output/input ratio, oranges are more energy-expensive to produce than apples. From the standpoint of vitamin C content, however, oranges with about 50 mg per 100 g are more valuable than apples, which contain 3 mg per 100 g.

Vegetables

'Vegetables' are the diverse parts of herbaceous plants consumed by man. Thus, cabbage and spinach are plant leaves; carrots, roots; broccoli, flowers; squash and tomato, fruits; peas and corn, seeds; onion, bulbs; and potato, tubers.

Table 8.2   Energy inputs in U.S. orange production.

	Quantity ha^{-1}	kcal ha^{-1}
Inputs		
Labour	173 h[a]	80 445[c]
Machinery	60 kg[a]	1 080 000[a]
Diesel	505 litres[b]	5 764 070
Gasoline	440 litres[b]	4 447 960
Nitrogen	195 kg[b]	2 866 500[d]
Phosphorus	46 kg[b]	138 000[d]
Potassium	188 kg[b]	300 800[d]
Limestone	45 kg[a]	14 175[d]
Irrigation	532 000 kcal[b]	532 000[b]
Insecticides	24 kg[b]	2 085 840[e]
Herbicides	0.2 kg[b]	19 982[e]
Fungicides	8 kg[b]	519 280[e]
Drying	—	—
Electricity	310 000 kcal[a]	310 000
Transportation	740 kg	190 180[f]
Total		18 349 232
Outputs		
Orange yield	19 040 kg[b]	6 778 240
kcal output/kcal input		0.37
Protein yield	190 kg	

(a) Estimated. (b) FEA, 1976a. (c) 173 h × 465 kcal h^{-1}. (d) See Appendix A. (e) See Appendix C. (f) 740 kg × 257 kcal kg^{-1}.

Vegetables are similar to fruits in their high water content, low fat and, except for beans and peas, low protein. Carbohydrate content, mainly starch, varies considerably from the high of about 22 % for lima beans to the low of 2 % for lettuce. Vegetables generally have a higher mineral and vitamin content than fruits. In particular, the dark green leafy vegetables like spinach are high in vitamin C, caro-tene and iron. Also, dark green leafy vegetables, except spinach and chard (goose foot family), are excellent sources of calcium. Oxalic acid in spinach may chemically bind some of the calcium, making it insoluble, hence less available to man. Many vegetables, especially seeds, are reliable sources of thiamine.

Selected for this energy analysis was a broad cross-section of veg-etables including: potato, spinach, Brussels sprouts, tomato, sugar beet and cassava.

Potato

The potato, or white potato, is one of the fifteen most common plant foods consumed by man in the world today. Even in the United States where a wide variety of vegetables is available, the potato is consumed in largest quantities. About 54 kg of potato are consumed per person per year or about 0.2 kg per day per person (USDA, 1975b).

Based on data from New York State, the greatest energy inputs in potato production are the fertilizers, which represent more than 1/3rd of the total input (Table 8.3). Another 1/3rd of the energy is expended for petroleum and machinery inputs that reduce the manpower input, which averages 35 hours per hectare.

Table 8.3 Energy inputs in New York State potato production.

	Quantity ha^{-1}	kcal ha^{-1}
Inputs		
Labour	35 h[a]	16 275[d]
Machinery	31 kg[b]	480 000
Diesel	152 litres[c]	1 734 928[e]
Gasoline	272 litres[c]	2 749 648[e]
Nitrogen	205 kg[a]	3 013 500[f]
Phosphorus	348 kg[a]	1 044 000
Potassium	198 kg[a]	316 800[f]
Seeds	1900 kg[a]	1 088 700[g]
Insecticides	31 kg[a]	2 694 210[h]
Herbicides	18 kg[a]	1 798 380[h]
Fungicides	6 kg[b]	389 460[a]
Electricity	47 kWh[c]	134 561[e]
Transportation	2249 kg	577 993[i]
Total		16 038 455
Outputs		
Potato yield	34 384 kg[a]	19 702 032
kcal output/kcal input		1.23
Protein yield	722 kg	

(a) Snyder, 1977. (b) Estimated. (c) FEA, 1976a. (d) 35 h ×465 kcal h^{-1}.
(e) See Appendix B. (f) See Appendix A. (g) 1900 kg ×573 kcal kg^{-1}.
(h) See Appendix C. (i) 2249 kg ×257 kcal kg^{-1}.

The total energy input for N.Y. potato production is 16.0×10^6 kcal ha^{-1}. From this energy input the potato yield is 19.7×10^6 kcal, resulting in an output/input ratio of 1.2:1, slightly lower than the 1.6:1 reported for the United Kingdom (Table 8.4) by Leach (1976). The differences in the inputs of the N.Y. and U.K. production are considered insignificant.

Although potatoes are only 2 % protein, the total yield of protein per hectare is substantial, amounting to 722 kg ha^{-1}. This is a relatively high yield, especially for a food so high in water content.

Table 8.4   Energy inputs in potato production in the United Kingdom (after Leach, 1976).

	Quantity ha^{-1}	kcal ha^{-1}
Inputs		
Field work, fuels for tractors (to harvest)	2.85 GJ	2.85
fuels for harvester, transport	3.38 GJ	3.38
Field work, tractor depreciation and repairs	1.14 GJ	1.14
harvester depreciation and repairs	6.70 GJ	6.70
Nitrogen	175 kg	14.00
Phosphorus	175 kg	2.45
Potassium	250 kg	2.25
Sprays	13 kg	1.24
Seed shed fuels (620 MJ/t seed)	1.57 GJ	1.57
Storage (1.65 kWh/net t)	0.57 GJ	0.57
Total		36.15
Outputs		
Potato yield	26 300 kg	56.9
kcal output/kcal input		1.57
Protein output	376 kg	

4186 J = 1 kcal.

Spinach

Spinach, a green leafy vegetable, is eaten raw or cooked. Although it is not a major vegetable throughout the world, it is nutritionally valuable. Like other dark green leafy vegetables, spinach contributes iron, riboflavin and vitamins A and C to the diet.

The largest energy input in U.S. spinach production is for nitrogen fertilizer, amounting to nearly 50 % of the total energy input (Table 8.5). The next largest inputs are for fuel and machinery. The energy inputs for production total 12.8×10^6 kcal ha^{-1} and the spinach yield is 2.9×10^6 kcal ha^{-1}. The output/input ratio is 0.2:1. This means that about 5 kcal of fossil energy are required for the production of each kcal of spinach.

Tomatoes

Botanically tomatoes are a fruit, but are included in this section because they are usually consumed as a vegetable. They are eaten in a variety of ways, including fresh in salads, cooked, canned and as juice. They are valued nutritionally for vitamin C (23 mg per 100 g of raw tomato), vitamin A and iron.

Based on data from tomato producers in California, 58 % of the energy inputs are for fuel and machinery that reduce labour inputs

Table 8.5 Energy inputs in U.S. spinach production (modified after Terhune, 1977).

	Quantity ha^{-1}	kcal ha^{-1}
Inputs		
Labour	56 h[a]	26 040[c]
Machinery	30 kg[b]	480 000
Fuel	297 litres[a]	2 970 000[a]
Nitrogen	470 kg[a]	6 909 000[d]
Phosphorus	354 kg[a]	1 062 000[d]
Potassium	136 kg[a]	217 600[d]
Limestone	454 kg[a]	143 010[d]
Seeds	33.6 kg[a]	135 300[a]
Irrigation	69 500 kcal[a]	69 500[a]
Insecticides	2 kg[a]	173 820[e]
Herbicides	2 kg[a]	199 820[e]
Electricity	300 000[a] kcal	300 000[a]
Transportation	287 kg	73 759[f]
Total		12 759 849
Outputs		
Spinach yield	11 200 kg[a]	2 912 000
kcal output/kcal input		0.23
Protein yield	358 kg[a]	

(a) Terhune, 1977. (b) Estimated. (c) 56 h ×465 kcal h^{-1}. (d) See Appendix A. (e) See Appendix C. (f) 1287 kg × 257 kcal kg^{-1}.

(Table 8.6). The second largest input is for fertilizers. The total energy input is 16.6 ×10^6 kcal ha^{-1} and the average tomato yield for California is 9.9 ×10^6 kcal. Based on this, the output/input ratio is about 0.6:1, or about 2 kcal of energy expended for every kcal tomato produced. Because the per hectare yield of tomatoes is so high, the protein yield of 496 kg ha^{-1} is also excellent even though tomatoes average only 1 % protein and have a high water content.

Brussels sprouts

Brussels sprouts are a favourite vegetable in the United Kingdom but seem less popular in the United States. Like spinach, they are an excellent source of vitamins A and C and iron.

As with most other vegetables, the major energy inputs for Brussels sprouts grown in the United States are for fuel and machinery, amounting to more than 1/3rd of the total input (Table 8.7). The next major input is for fertilizers. The total energy input for Brussels sprouts production is 8.1 ×10^6 kcal ha^{-1}.

Balanced against this input is the yield of about 5.5 ×10^6 kcal of food energy. Hence, the output/input ratio is 0.7:1. Although

Table 8.6   Energy inputs in California tomato production.

	Quantity ha^{-1}	kcal ha^{-1}
Inputs		
Labour	165 h[a]	76 725[e]
Machinery	30 kg[b]	480 000
Diesel	246 litres[c]	2 807 844[f]
Gasoline	628 litres[c]	6 348 452[f]
Nitrogen	168 kg[d]	2 469 600[g]
Phosphorus	56 kg[d]	168 000[g]
Potassium	96 kg[b]	153 600[g]
Limestone	50 kg[b]	15 750[g]
Seeds	4 kg[b]	20 000[b]
Irrigation	1 010 900 kcal[c]	1 010 900[c]
Insecticides	25 kg[a]	2 172 525[h]
Herbicides	2 kg[a]	199 820[h]
Fungicides	4 kg[b]	259 640[h]
Electricity	200 000 kcal[b]	200 000[b]
Transportation	691 kg	177 587[i]
Total		16 560 443
Outputs		
Tomato yield	49 616 kg[a]	9 923 200
kcal output/kcal input		0.60
Protein yield	496 kg	

(a) Walker and Hunt, 1973. (b) Estimated. (c) FEA, 1976a. (d) Cervinka *et al.*, 1974. (e) 165 h ×465 kcal h^{-1}. (f) See Appendix B. (g) See Appendix A. (h) See Appendix C. (i) 1691 kg ×257 kcal kg^{-1}.

Table 8.7   Energy inputs in U.S. Brussels sprouts production.

	Quantity ha^{-1}	kcal ha^{-1}
Inputs		
Labour	60 h[a]	27 900[c]
Machinery	30 kg[b]	480 000
Fuel	285 litres[a]	2 881 065[d]
Nitrogen	180 kg[a]	2 646 000[e]
Phosphorus	45 kg[a]	135 000[e]
Potassium	40 kg[a]	64 000[e]
Limestone	40 kg[a]	12 600[e]
Seeds	4 kg[a]	16 120[a]
Insecticides	5 kg[a]	434 550[f]
Herbicides	10 kg[a]	999 100[f]
Electricity	300 000 kcal[b]	300 000[b]
Transportation	249 kg	63 993[g]
Total		8 060 328
Outputs		
Brussels sprouts yield	12 320 kg[a]	5 544 000
kcal output/kcal input		0.69
Protein yield	604 kg	

(a) Pimentel, 1976. (b) Estimated. (c) 60 h ×465 kcal h^{-1}. (d) See Appendix B. (e) See Appendix A. (f) See Appendix C. (g) 249 kg ×257 kcal kg^{-1}.

Brussels sprouts do not yield either as much food energy or protein per hectare as potatoes, the average yield of 604 kg protein per hectare is significant. Of the vegetables analyzed for their output/input ratio, Brussels sprouts place second to potatoes in high yield of calories and protein per hectare.

Sugar beet

The sugar beet is another plant that is not generally classed as a vegetable, but is included in this section because it is a valuable food commodity in many parts of the world. Both sugar beets and sugar-cane contain sucrose. Although the sweetener is valued for its energy, it contributes no vitamins, minerals or protein.

A major advantage of sugar beets over sugar-cane is that they can be grown in temperate regions, whereas sugar-cane can only be produced in tropical or subtropical regions.

Based on data from Leach (1976), about 50 % of the energy input for sugar beet production in the United Kingdom is for nitrogen fertilizer (Table 8.8). Machinery and fuel require the second largest energy inputs.

The beet yield averages 35 500 kg ha^{-1} and contains about 16.5 % sugar for processing. For sugar alone, the output/input ratio is about 3.6:1, one of the more efficient output/input ratios for the crops analyzed in this section.

Tables 8.8 Energy inputs for sugar beet production in the United Kingdom (after Leach, 1976).

	Quantity/ha	GJ/ha
Inputs		
Field work, tractor fuels (to harvest)	2.50 GJ	2.50
harvester, transport fuels	2.54 GJ	2.54
Field work, tractor depreciation +repairs (total)	2.00 GJ	2.00
harvester depreciation +repairs	2.80 GJ	2.80
Nitrogen	160 kg	12.80
Phosphorus	50 kg	0.70
Potassium	150 kg	1.35
NaCl	70 kg	0.10
Kainit (17 % K$_2$O)	280 kg	0.43
Sprays	10.9 kg	1.09
Seed	£7.5 ×144 MJ/£	1.08
Total		27.39
Outputs		
Sugar beet yield	35 500 kg	99.1
kcal output/kcal input		3.62

4186 J = 1 kcal.

Cassava

Cassava, based on available energy output/input data, is an important crop (Table 8.9). The data for cassava production presented
here are from the Tanga Region of Africa. Cassava grown in that
region has the efficient output/input ratio of 23:1.

Table 8.9 Energy inputs in the Tanga Region of Africa for cassava
production.

	Quantity ha^{-1}	kcal ha^{-1}
Inputs		
Labour	1284 h[a]	821 760[c]
Hoe	16 500 kcal[b]	16 500[b]
Stem cuttings	none	–
Total		838 260
Outputs		
Cassava yield	5824 kg	19 219 200
kcal output/kcal input		22.93
Protein yield	58 kg	

(a) Ruthenberg, 1968. (b) Estimated. (c) On a per day basis the manpower
energy input is: (1) 8 hours of work at 350 kcal h^{-1}; (2) 6 hours of other
activities at 145 kcal h^{-1}; and (3) 10 hours of rest at 45 kcal h^{-1}. This
totals 4120 kcal input per person.

The root of the cassava shrub is harvested 9–12 months after the
planting of the stem cuttings. About 1300 hours of labour per hectare are required for the production of the crop. Total energy input
is calculated at about 838 300 kcal ha^{-1}, and the yield is about
19.2×10^6 kcal ha^{-1}. This high energy yield comes mainly from the
starch component of cassava. The protein yield, however is a low 58
kg ha^{-1}. Furthermore the quality of cassava protein is considered
the lowest of all plant proteins. With cassava production so efficient
and the plant generally acceptable as food, it is unfortunate that the
quality and quantity of protein is so inadequate.

Forage Production

Forage production is an essential part of most livestock production
systems, especially for ruminant animals. As with all types of crop
production systems, energy inputs are necessary for the production
of forage crops. In general, these systems are not intensively
managed because forage crops on a per land area basis have a
relatively low monetary return.

Alfalfa, tame hay and corn silage productions were analyzed to estimate the energy input/output ratios that are typical in forage production.

Alfalfa

Alfalfa is not only one of the most productive forages but also one of the most nutritious for livestock.

Because it is fairly typical, the data from Ohio were analyzed. There the major inputs in alfalfa production, as with most intensive cropping systems, are for fuel and machinery (Table 8.10). Together these total about 70 % of the input in alfalfa production. In contrast to most other crops, little or no nitrogen fertilizer is needed, for alfalfa like legumes is associated with nitrogen-fixing bacteria. Since nitrogen fertilizer is an energy-costly input, this helps keep alfalfa production relatively energy efficient.

Table 8.10 Energy inputs in Ohio alfalfa production.

	Quantity ha^{-1}	kcal ha^{-1}
Inputs		
Labour	13 h[a]	6045[c]
Machinery	20 kg[b]	360 000
Gasoline	129 litres[a]	1 304 061[d]
Nitrogen	7 kg[a]	103 900[e]
Phosphorus	45 kg[a]	135 000[e]
Potassium	59 kg[a]	94 400[e]
Limestone	179 kg[a]	56 385[e]
Seeds	4.5 kg[a]	279 000[f]
Insecticides	0.4 kg[a]	34 764[g]
Herbicides	0.2 kg[a]	19 982[g]
Electricity	26 kWh[a]	74 438[h]
Transportation	132 kg	33 924[i]
Total		2 501 899
Outputs		
Alfalfa yield	6832 kg[a]	15 440 320
kcal output/kcal input		6.17
Protein yield	1127 kg	

(a) USDA, 1977b. (b) Estimated. (c) 13 h ×465 kcal h^{-1}. (d) See Appendix B. (e) See Appendix A. (f) Heichel, 1978. (g) See Appendix C. (h) See Appendix B. (i) 132 kg ×257 kcal kg^{-1}.

The total energy input for alfalfa production is calculated to be 2.5×10^6 kcal ha^{-1}. With a yield of about 15.4×10^6 kcal, the output/input ratio is 6:1.

In addition to energy yield, alfalfa provides about 1100 kg protein per hectare, considered a high protein yield. Of importance is the fact that alfalfa supplies a major share of the plant protein fed to animals in the United States.

Tame hay

The major forage feed for cattle, sheep, and other ruminants in the world is tame hay consisting of numerous grass species. Animals are allowed to graze the hay as it grows in the pasture and do the harvesting themselves. Some of the hay is harvested by man and it is this production system that is analyzed here.

As with alfalfa, two major inputs for tame hay production in the United States are for fuel and machinery (Table 8.11). Together these two inputs account for about 42 % of the total energy expended for production.

Table 8.11   Energy inputs in U.S. tame hay production.

	Quantity ha[-1]	kcal ha[-1]
Inputs		
Labour	16 h[a]	7440[d]
Machinery	20 kg[b]	360 000
Fuel	36 litres[c]	363 924[e]
Nitrogen	7 kg[c]	102 900[f]
Phosphorus	8 kg[c]	24 000[f]
Potassium	16 kg[c]	25 600[f]
Limestone	15 kg[b]	4725[f]
Seeds	30 kg[a]	630 000[g]
Herbicides	1 kg[c]	99 910[h]
Electricity	75 000 kcal[b]	75 000[b]
Transportation	88 kg	22 616[i]
Total		1 716 115
Outputs		
Tame hay yield	5000 kg[a]	8 578 680
kcal output/kcal input		5.0
Protein yield	200 kg	

(a) Pimentel, 1976. (b) Estimated. (c) FEA, 1976a. (d) 16 ×465 kcal kg[-1]. (e) See Appendix B. (f) See Appendix A. (g) Heichel, 1978. (h) See Appendix C. (i) 88 kg ×257 kcal kg[-1].

The average yield is estimated to be about 8.6×10^6 kcal ha[-1] in forage feed energy. Balanced against the total energy input of about 1.7×10^6 kcal ha[-1], the energy output/input ratio is 5:1 for U.S. tame hay production.

Note that the 5:1 ratio for the United States is a better return than the 2:1 ratio reported for production in the United Kingdom (Table 8.12). This is because, although the yields in the United Kingdom are more than double those in the United States, the nitrogen input used in the United Kingdom is more than 30 times that in the United States.

Table 8.12 Energy inputs for tame hay production for a typical U.K. production system (after Leach, 1976).

	Quantity ha^{-1}	GJ ha^{-1}
Inputs		
Field work, fuels	2.57 GJ	2.57
Field work, machinery	3.53 GJ	3.53
Nitrogen	250 kg	21.62
Total		27.7
Outputs		
Hay yield	10 300 kg	65.5
kcal output/kcal input		2.36

4186 J = 1 kcal.

Another less intensive hay production system in the United Kingdom yielded a more favourable ratio of 6:1 compared to 2:1 for the intensive system (Table 8.13).

Table 8.13 Energy inputs in tame hay production in a relatively efficient U.K. production system (after Leach, 1976).

	Quantity ha^{-1}	GJ ha^{-1}
Inputs		
Field work (machinery)	2.0 GJ	2.00
Nitrogen	80 kg	7.48
Total		9.48
Outputs		
Hay yield	5600 kg	53.0
kcal output/kcal input		5.6

4186 J = 1 kcal.

Corn silage

Corn silage consist of mature corn plants that are cut green, chopped, and then stored in a silo. During storage the chopped corn ferments and this process helps preserve it. In U.S. production systems the total energy inputs for silage production average 6.3 ×10⁶ kcal ha⁻¹ (Table 8.14). Even with 70 % moisture, yields of corn silage are high, averaging about 25.3 ×10⁶ kcal. Thus the output/input ratio for corn silage is 4:1 or significantly greater than the 3:1 output/input ratio for corn grain.

Table 8.14   Energy inputs per hectare in New York corn silage production.

	Quantity ha⁻¹	kcal ha⁻¹
Inputs		
Labour	15 h[a]	6975[a]
Machinery	40 kg[b]	720 000
Diesel	110 litres[c]	1 255 540[e]
Gasoline	105 litres[c]	1 071 554[e]
Nitrogen	116 kg[a]	1 705 200[f]
Phosphorus	66 kg[a]	198 000[f]
Potassium	75 kg[a]	120 000[f]
Limestone	560 kg[a]	176 400[f]
Seeds	19 kg[a]	475 000[g]
Insecticides	2.5 kg[a]	217 275[h]
Herbicides	2.5 kg[a]	249 775[h]
Electricity	12 kWh[c]	34 356[i]
Transportation	211 kg	54 227[j]
Total		6 284 302
Outputs		
Corn silage yield	31 020 kg[a]	25 284 402
kcal output/kcal input		4.02
Protein yield	393 kg	

(a) Snyder, 1976. (b) Estimated. (c) FEA, 1976a. (d) 15 h ×465 kcal h⁻¹.
(e) See Appendix B. (f) See Appendix A. (g) Heichel, 1978. (h) See Appendix C. (i) See Appendix B. (j) 211 kg × 257 kcal kg⁻¹.

Vegetarianism and Non-vegetarianism and Energy Inputs

So far in Chapters 6–8, energy inputs for the production of various animal and plant foods have been analyzed. The question then arises as to what the fossil fuel requirements would be for types of typical human diets made up of various combinations of animal and plant foods. In other words, are some types of diets more conserving of fossil energy than others? Humans seldom eat just one or two foods but instead make dietary choices from a variety of available foods. Basically, however, eating patterns can be classified as to the type of protein eaten. These are the non-vegetarian diets that include both animal and plant proteins, often as in the United States, with a predomination of animal protein. In another called the lacto–ovo diet, eggs, milk and milk products comprise the only animal protein eaten while in the complete vegetarian diet no animal proteins are eaten.

The following example illustrates some of the differences in fossil fuel requirements of these various dietary regimes.

For these calculations data from the United States are used. The average daily food intake is 3300 kcal (USDA, 1977b) and is held constant for the three diets. The amount of protein is over 100 g per day in the nonvegetarian diet and declines to about 80 g in the all vegetarian diet.

Nearly twice as much fossil energy is expended for the food in a lacto-ovo vegetarian diet than the pure vegetarian (Fig. 8.1). For the non-vegetarian diet, the fossil energy input is more than three-fold that of the pure vegetarian diet.

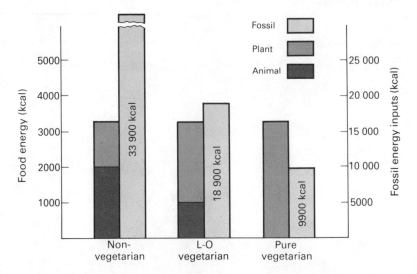

Fig. 8.1 Daily food energy intake of pure vegetarians, lacto-ovo vegetarians (L–O), and non-vegetarians and the calculated fossil energy inputs to produce these diets under U.S. conditions.

Based on these sample calculations, the pure vegetarian diet is more economical in terms of fossil energy than either of the other two types of diets. Of course energy expenditure is not the only factor to be evaluated when dietary choices are made. Personal choices are often made based on desired palatability characteristics of a food. In addition, there can be significant nutritional difference between the pure vegetarian diet and those that include animal products. Of importance is the fact that vitamin B_{12}, an essential nutrient, is lacking in pure vegetarian diets and must be taken as a dietary supplement. Further, the quality of protein may vary depending on the combination of plant proteins consumed. When the essential amino acids of the plant food are complemented, then protein quality of a vegetarian diet will be satisfactory. A diet of all plant foods is usually of greater volume and bulk, making it difficult for young children and women to consume the quantities necessary to meet all nutritional needs. In addition, nutritionally vulnerable groups such as infants, rapidly growing adolescents, and pregnant and lactating women may need nutritional supplements of vitamins A and D, and iodine while on a pure vegetarian diet.

When we are faced with considering options for the future, the fact that producing plant food is significantly more energy efficient deserves consideration in agricultural policy as well as personal dietary choices.

9 Energy Use in Fish Production

A wide variety of freshwater and salt-water fishes, crustaceans and molluscs serve as food for man. Between 60 and 70 $\times 10^6$ tonnes of seafood, including fishes, crustaceans, and molluscs, are harvested annually from the oceans (Fig. 9.1). This represents about 95 % of all fish harvested and utilized by man. The other 5 % is freshwater fish.

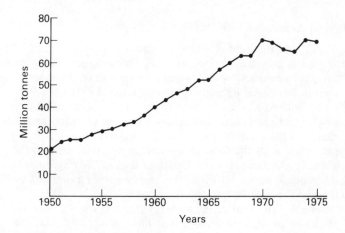

Fig. 9.1 World fish catch (FAO, 1976).

Nearly 1/3rd of all harvested fish (about 20 $\times 10^6$ tonnes) is fed to livestock (FAO, 1973; Brown and Eckholm, 1974). Only an estimated 6 $\times 10^6$ tonnes are directly consumed by man (Pimentel *et al.*, 1975). Thus, fish protein represents only about 5 % of man's total annual food protein (122 $\times 10^6$ tonnes) consumption.

Serious over-fishing of the common fishes already exists in many parts of the world (Brown and Eckholm, 1974; Brown *et al.*, 1976) and increased pressure on the fish populations appears to be the worldwide trend. For example, the gradual increase in fish yield between 1950 and 1970 has been followed by a sharp decline (Fig.

9.1). Although this decline was in part related to a reduction of the anchovy populations off the coast of Peru, a main cause was simply over-fishing of the world fisheries. Since 1973, however, anchovy fishing off Peru has improved and this has improved total yields.

Perhaps fish production could be improved or managed more efficiently to add more fish protein to the human food supply. For example, trash fish, which usually are discarded or used as animal feed, could be used more effectively. Also small crustaceans such as krill are now beginning to be used for food. So perhaps by combining the more effective utilization of trash fish and krill, with sound fishery management and increased cooperation among nations, the annual fish harvests could be increased to 100×10^6 tonnes of fish protein. However, if the total world population nearly doubles in the next 25 years, as expected, the percentage of the world protein diet supplied by fish will remain at the present level or less than 5% (Pimentel *et al.*, 1975).

Ecological Aspects of Fish Production

About 0.03% of the light reaching an aquatic ecosystem is fixed by aquatic plants, primarily phytoplankton. The amount of light fixed is calculated to be about 4×10^6 kcal ha^{-1} per year, or about 1/3rd that fixed in terrestrial habitats (Pimentel *et al.*, 1978).

The phytoplankton that fix light energy in the ocean are eaten by zooplankton. After passing through 4–6 links in the food chain, the light energy is then harvested as fish. With the transfer of energy through each link in the food chain, energy is dissipated and the final quantity available is much less than that at the phytoplankton level. In general, about 1/10th of the energy entering one link is passed on to the next link in the food chain.

Assuming 4×10^6 kcal of light energy per hectare per year are fixed in the ocean ecosystem, and four links in a food chain, the energy harvestable as fish would be about 400 kcal ha^{-1} per year. Measured in weight of fish this amounts to only 0.15 kg harvested per hectare per year.

If the 115 kg of meat consumed per person per year in the United States were to be supplied by fish from the oceans, and assuming a 0.15 kg yield per hectare, about 1924 ha of ocean area per person would be necessary. This estimate assumes that the entire yield is suitable for human food and that 40% of it would be edible meat. Actually, man eats only a few species of fish. This example emphasizes that one of the major problems inherent in increasing fish production is searching many square kilometres of ocean for suitable fish species. It is this searching process, often far from port, that makes fishing operations so energy intensive.

Ocean Fisheries

The major equipment used in harvesting ocean fish are vessels and the diverse gear needed to search for, capture and transport the fish. Both the construction and operation of this equipment consumes energy. Although the fishing vessels also require manpower as crew, this is not a large energy input, especially on the new, heavily mechanized fishing vessels of today.

The energy input in several different fishing systems is examined below, with more detailed analysis made of the fishery in the northeastern United States.

Northeast U.S. fishery

The location of large fish populations along the continental shelf in the northeastern United States has made this one of the most productive fishery regions of the world. As with all food producing systems, energy must be invested in the form of equipment, fuel and labour.

Because fishing in this region is done in different ways, this analysis is divided into two categories: (1) the inshore pelagic system that utilizes small fishing vessels weighing less than 110 GRT (gross registered tons); and (2) the offshore fishing system that employs larger vessels weighing more than 110 GRT. For the inshore pelagic fishery, an input of only 1.03 kcal of fossil energy is required to harvest 1 kcal of fish protein (Table 9.1). The offshore fishery requires an input of 3.9 kcal of fossil energy per kcal of fish protein harvested. Thus, smaller fishing units are nearly four times as efficient as those fishing greater distances offshore. The lower energy

Table 9.1 Current energy effort situation in the Northeast fishing zone (Rochereau and Pimentel, 1978).

	kcal fossil energy input/kcal of fish protein total output[b]	kcal fossil energy input/kcal of fish protein output for humans[c]
Average for Total system	1.65	4.10
Inshore Sub-system[d]	1.03	2.18
Offshore (oceanic) Sub-system[a]	3.90	9.55

(a) Including the rest of the fishing fleet $\geq$ 110 GRT capacity per fishing unit. (b) Includes total harvest of fish protein including trash fish. (c) Fish protein harvested and used as only human food. (d) Including the fishing units $\leq$ 110 GRT capacity.

ratios for the inshore fishery are due in part to the greater
productivity of the inshore region. The inshore species are mainly
zooplankton-eating fish species, and they are about 1/3rd more
efficient than the offshore fishes in storing energy per weight of
useable biomass (Rochereau and Pimentel, 1978). The offshore
fishes are primarily carnivorous and are higher up in the food chain.

If the trash fish were removed from the reported fish yields, the
overall efficiency of the Northeast fishery in producing fish protein
suitable for human consumption decreases, as evidenced by the
average output/input ratio of 4.1 kcal of fossil energy per kcal of
human fish protein output (Fig. 9.2). Specifically, the inshore fishery
requires about 2.2 kcal of fossil energy per kcal of fish protein
produced, whereas the offshore fishery requires 9.6 kcal of energy
per kcal of fish protein output (Table 9.1).

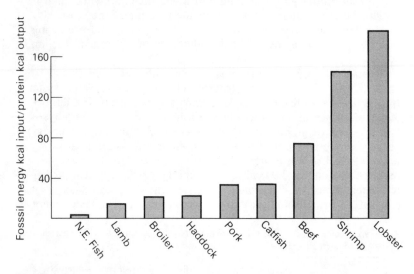

Fig. 9.2 Fossil energy inputs per protein energy output for various fishery and several livestock systems.

The relatively high efficiency of Northeast fishery is evident when
compared with other fishery systems. Considering the entire U.S.
fisheries industry, Hirst (1974) reported that about 27 kcal of fossil
energy input are required to harvest 1 kcal of fish protein. Leach
(1976) in the United Kingdom reported about 20 kcal of fossil
energy input per kcal of fish protein output, and Edwardson (1975)
reported that steel trawlers operating from Scotland use about 21
kcal of energy per kcal of fish protein harvested. He also reported
that the wooden vessels used for inshore fishing require only 2.1

kcal of fossil energy input per kcal of fish protein output. This agrees favourably with the 2.2 kcal fossil energy input for the inshore Northeast fishery (Table 9.1).

A major reason for the high efficiency of the Northeast fishing system is that about 93 % of the fishing vessel fleet is relatively small, between 5 and 150 GRT. The advantage of using small fishing vessels for fishing is illustrated by the following example. Assume an annual yield for the Northeast fishery of 7.6×10^{11} kcal of fish protein and an overall regional fishing capacity of 7×10^4 GRT, which is typical of the Northeast conditions today. If a 300 GRT fleet of vessels were employed instead of the usual small vessels, the input/output ratio would rise from the present 4.1 to about 6.7 kcal of fossil energy input per kcal of fish protein harvested (Rochereau and Pimentel, 1978). This would represent a 63 % decline in fishing efficiency.

Overall efficiency declines as the size of fishing vessels increases because a non-linear relationship exists between vessel size and the gross energy requirements of these vessels (Fig. 9.3). For example, 22 vessels of 15 GRT have the same capacity as one 330 GRT vessel; yet the smaller vessels in total are 44 % more energy efficient in obtaining the same fish yield output. For all vessel types, the inputs for operating the vessels are the largest of the three inputs and in the small vessels (7–15 GRT), operation inputs significantly dominate the inputs. Note that although operation dominates the

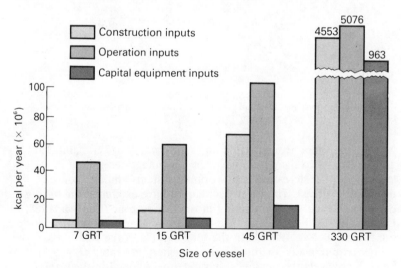

Fig. 9.3 Annual energy inputs for construction, operation, and capital equipment for various sizes of vessels fishing in the Northeast region (after Rochereau and Pimentel, 1978).

inputs in the larger vessels, construction also becomes a major input.

U.S. government policies continue to support the trend to launch larger vessels for use in the rich Northeast fishery grounds. Such vessels do use less labour, but unfortunately they are far less efficient in fossil energy use than are the smaller vessels. Surely this is a questionable policy in view of rising fossil fuel prices and unemployment in the industrial world.

The energy efficiency of the Northeast fishing fleet has been declining steadily since the early 1960s (Fig. 9.4), a decline attributed both to the upsurge of international fishing competition on the

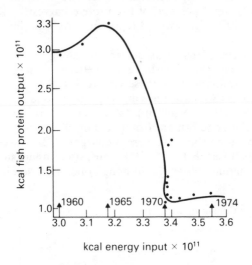

Fig. 9.4 Change in the fossil energy input (kcal) per kcal fish protein output for the Northeast fishery system during the past 15 years (after Rochereau and Pimentel, 1978).

Northeast fishery grounds (Bell and Hazleton, 1967; Gulland, 1971 and 1974) and to the development of new integrated fishing technology (i.e. stern-trawling hydraulic systems and electronic detection systems). These new techniques have expanded the fishing capacity of each vessel operating in the fishing zone (Captiva, 1968; DeFever, 1968; FAO, 1972a; Gulland, 1974; Margetts, 1974). For the period 1960 to 1964, both the total GRT and the total gross energy requirements for the Northeast fishery increased (Fig. 9.5). Since 1964 a relative steadiness has been maintained in the total gross energy requirements while the total GRT has declined sharply. The steadiness in the total gross energy requirements reflects

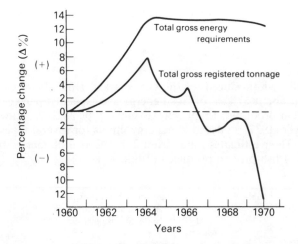

Fig. 9.5 Percentage change in total gross energy requirements (GER) and the total gross register tonnage (GRT) of fishing vessels from 1960 to 1970 in Northeast fishery (after Rochereau and Pimentel, 1978).

replacement of smaller vessels with fewer but larger vessels that require more energy both to construct and operate.

Another factor contributing to the deterioration of the Northeast fishery is that the coastal water zone is currently being over-fished; that is, the harvest is well above the maximum sustained yield level of the area. Large harvests continue because the fishing system in this region has the capital equipment to maintain this high level of exploitation (Bell and Hazleton, 1967; Henry, 1971; Gulland, 1971; FAO, 1972b; USDC, 1974). Many scientists believe that there is no extra biological stock to act as a buffer to the large fish harvests.

The decline in fish protein production and the increase in fossil energy input (Fig. 9.4) has been associated with a decline in investment return of a typical 50 GRT trawler during the 1967–1974 period (Rochereau, 1976). Based on the annual operating cost figures, which reflect the level of seasonal activity (Bell and Hazleton, 1967), an inverse relationship exists between the return on the investment and the level of fishing effort in the Northeast fishery region. That is, as the amount of fishing done increases, the return in money decreases. Indeed, the Northeast fishery system appears to be approaching a time when the catch will cover only operating costs, and the operation will run in the red. This is evidenced by comparing returns on investment indices. In 1973, the deflated return on investment index was more than 5 times less than in 1968 for a similar level of effort (Rochereau, 1976). The combined effects of overfishing, rising costs and variable earnings account for the economic instability and the gradual deterioration of the Northeast fishing industry.

U.S. fishery

For all the fish produced for the U.S. market, Hirst (1974) calculated that about 27 kcal of fossil energy are expended per kcal of fish protein produced. Employing a similar type analysis, Rawitscher and Mayer (1977) analyzed the energy inputs for several types of seafood. Their estimates range from 2 to 192 kcal of energy input per kcal of fish protein produced (Table 9.2).

Table 9.2   Energy Input for the Production of Various Seafood in the United States (Calculated from data of Rawitscher and Mayer, 1977).

Seafood type	kcal fossil energy input/ kcal output of protein
Herring	2
Perch, ocean	4
Salmon, pink	8
Cod	20
Tuna	20
Haddock	23
Halibut	23
Salmon, king	40
Shrimp	150
Lobster	192

The most efficient fish protein produced is herring, with only 2 kcal of fossil energy needed to produce 1 kcal of herring protein. A common fish such as haddock requires an input of 23 kcal of fossil energy per output protein kcal. The largest input is 192 kcal of fossil energy per kcal of lobster protein produced. This high cost for the production of lobster protein is not surprising considering the scarcity of lobsters and the extensive fishing effort that goes into harvesting these animals.

Peru (anchovy)

The anchovy fishing grounds off Peru are one of the most productive fisheries anywhere. The fish meal and other fish products produced from this fishery are shipped to many parts of the world. In particular, Europe and the United States import large amounts of anchovy fish meal for use in poultry and other livestock production systems.

Leach (1976) gathered data on anchoveta and fish meal production. However, the inputs in this analysis included only those for petroleum. No inputs were included for construction of the vessels, for equipment, and fishing gear. As indicated by data from the Northeast fishery system, these inputs are substantial and often represent about 1/2 of the total energy inputs in a fishery system (Rochereau and Pimentel, 1978).

An analysis of the inputs needed to produce 1 kg of anchovy suggests that about 2 kcal of petroleum are necessary to produce 1 kcal of fish protein (Table 9.3). This input is more than twice that of 1.03 kcal of fossil energy needed to produce a kilogram of inshore fish protein products in the Northeast fishery (Tables 9.1 and 9.3). If construction and maintenance of vessels and gear were included in the Peruvian fish production data, fish production in the inshore Northeast fishery area would be 6 times more efficient than the anchovy industry.

Table 9.3 Energy inputs for anchoveta and fish meal production off Peru (fuel inputs only) (after Leach, 1976).

	GJ/tonne
Inputs	
Catching 6.56 tonne fish, 0.54 GJ tonne^{-1}	3.00
Large fish meal plant, 18 % conversion to meal, 11.8 GJ/tonne	11.80
Sub-total at factory gate	14.80
Shipping 11 600 km to UK, 0.2 MJ tonne^{-1} km^{-1} on one way trip	2.30
Total	17
Outputs	
1 tonne meal plus approx. 0.1 tonne fish oils; protein content of meal 60 %, oils negligible.	
Protein 1 tonne	28.5
kcal input/kcal output	1.67:1

4186 J = 1 kcal.

Gulf of Mexico (shrimp)

By comparison with herring, haddock and anchovies, the production of shrimp in the Gulf of Mexico requires large inputs of energy, or 206 kcal of fossil energy expended per kcal of shrimp protein produced (Table 9.4). Also, this ratio is higher than the average of 150 kcal energy input per kcal of shrimp protein produced in the United States (Table 9.2).

Although producing shrimp in the Gulf of Mexico is energy intensive, this does not mean that the investment is uneconomical at

Table 9.4   Energy inputs for shrimp production in the Gulf of Mexico (fuel input only) (after Leach, 1976).

	GJ/tonne
Inputs	
8300 litres or 6.95 tonne gas-oil per tonne shrimps landed:	
total to dockside	3.59
Outputs	
1 tonne shrimp, 65 % edible weight, 3.38 MJ kg^{-1}	
and 16 % protein edible portion	
Protein 104 kg	1.74
kcal input/kcal output	206.32

4186 J = 1 kcal.

present. Shrimps are an extremely valuable seafood, and the dollar return is currently high enough to offset the cost of energy expended and other production costs.

Australia (shrimp)

In Australia, only 22 kcal of fossil energy input are needed to produce 1 kcal of shrimp protein (Table 9.5). This is also significantly less than the U.S. average of 150 kcal and the Gulf of Mexico average of 206 kcal fossil energy input per kcal of shrimp protein harvested.

Table 9.5   Energy inputs for shrimp production off Australia (after Leach, 1976).

	GJ/tonne
Inputs	
573 litres or 0.48 tonne gas-oil per tonne shrimps landed	24.5
Vessel maintenance, £105 per tonne landed ×90 MJ £$^{-1}$	9.5
Vessel manufacture, £41.8 per tonne landed ×90 MJ £$^{-1}$	3.8
Total to dockside	38.1
Outputs	
1 tonne shrimp, 65 % edible weight, 3.38 MJ kg^{-1} and	
16 % protein edible portion	
Protein 104 g	1.74
kcal input/kcal output	21.90

4186 J = 1 kcal.

Malta (all types of fish)

The Malta fishing industry reported an input of 25 kcal of fossil energy per kcal of fish protein produced (Table 9.6). This input/output ratio of 25:1 is similar to the 27:1 reported for the U.S. fishery and also to the 20:1 of the U.K. fishery (Hirst, 1974; Leach, 1976).

Table 9.6 Energy inputs for fish production off Malta (fuel input only) (after Leach, 1976)

	GJ/tonne
Inputs	
0.78 tonne diesel fuel per tonne fish landed	40.3
Outputs	
1 tonne fish, assumed 60 % edible, 2.9 MJ kg^{-1} and 16 % protein edible portion	
Protein 96 kg	1.61
kcal input/kcal output	25.05

4186 J = 1 kcal.

Adriatic (all types of fish)

An analysis of fish production in the Adriatic region indicates that this fishery system is energy intensive. When small vessels capable of harvesting 50 tonnes of fish per vessel per year are used, the average energy input is about 68 kcal of energy per kcal of fish protein produced (Table 9.7). However, when large vessels capable of harvesting 150 tonnes of fish per vessel per year are used, energy

Table 9.7 Energy inputs for fish production in the Adriatic (fuel input only) (after Leach, 1976).

	GJ/tonne	
Inputs		
Small vessels: 2.1 tonne fuel per tonne fish landed	109	
Large vessels: 3.3 tonne fuel per tonne fish landed	170	
Outputs		
1 tonne fish, assumed 60 % edible, 2.9 MJ kg^{-1} and 16 % protein edible portion		
Protein yield 96 kg (1.61 GJ)		
	Small vessels	*Large vessels*
Energy as protein	109 GJ	170 GJ
kcal input/kcal output ratio	67.70	105.59

4186 J = 1 kcal.

input increases to about 100 kcal of fossil energy per kcal of fish protein produced. The relative efficiencies of small versus large vessels are similar to those of vessels used in the U.S. Northeast fishery industry, where the smaller vessels are four times as efficient as the large vessels (Rochereau, 1976).

Aquaculture

Aquaculture of fish is receiving serious attention with the hope that more high quality protein can be produced in this way. In the southern United States, catfish aquaculture is practiced on a commerical scale. Catfish is an excellent eating fish, but at this time it is relatively unknown outside of the southern States.

The largest energy input in catfish aquaculture is the feed. Westoby and Kase (1974) and Mack (1971) report a total of 5.9 tonnes of feed are fed to catfish over the 1.5 years necessary to reach marketable weight of 0.5 kg per fish (Table 9.8). The total fossil energy input for the production of catfish feed is 39×10^6 kcal. The other major input for this system is 9.5×10^6 kcal for production and maintenance of equipment. An additional 4.3×10^6 kcal is expended in pumping and circulating the water in the 4-ha ponds.

Table 9.8   Energy inputs for commercial catfish production in hectare ponds in Louisiana (after Westoby and Kase, 1974; Mack, 1971).

	Quantity ha^{-1}	kcal ha^{-1}
Inputs		
Labour	120 h	63 250
Equipment	9 500 000 kcal	9 500 000
Pumping	1667 kWh	4 343 250
Fertilizer and		
other chemicals	3.3 kg	60 000
Feed	5925 kg	39 000 000
Total		52 500 500
Outputs		
Catfish yield	2783 kg	
kcal input/kcal output ratio		34.2
Protein yield	384 kg*	1 536 000

* Assuming a dressed weight of 60 % and 23 % protein in the catfish fillet.

The total inputs to produce the yield of about 2780 kg of catfish per hectare are 52.5×10^6 kcal of fossil energy. Assuming a 60 % dressed weight and 23 % protein, the total production of catfish protein is 384 kg.

The 384 kg of catfish protein is the equivalent of 1.5×10^6 kcal of food energy. Thus, the input/output ratio is calculated to be 34 kcal of fossil energy input per kcal of catfish protein produced.

This ratio is similar to that of another catfish production system that has an input/output ratio of 35:1 (Pimentel *et al.*, 1975). The catfish input/output ratio is remarkably similar to the 35:1 for U.S. pork production (35:1) (Pimentel *et al.*, 1975).

Although catfish are cold-blooded and use no energy in heating their bodies, they are not particularly efficient in converting feed into protein. Specifically, they are much less efficient than broilers, for example, that require an input of 22 kcal of fossil energy input to produce 1 kcal of broiler protein, but are more efficient than beef, shrimp, and lobster (Fig. 9.2).

Conclusion

Fish production in a system like the Northeast system is quite economical in terms of energy inputs. In contrast, other fishery production, like shrimp and lobster, have extremely high energy inputs (Fig. 9.2). Compared to livestock production systems, fishery products have about the same range of energy inputs.

Obviously, much research needs to be done if the full potential of fish as human food is to be developed. Species of fish acceptable to humans, type of vessels used, control of fish harvest, and culturing species are but some of the areas that merit further study. Even if fish production could be improved, the rapid population growth rate will tend to negate the effect of greater yields.

10 Food Processing, Packaging and Preparation

Food processing

Ever since man first controlled fire he has used its heat to cook some of his foods. Cooking, either by roasting, baking, steaming, frying, broiling or boiling, makes many foods more palatable. Indeed, the flavour of such foods as meat is enhanced by cooking. The flavour and consistency of many cereals are improved and their carbohydrate content is made more digestible when they are heated. Although not all vegetables are cooked before eating, the heating process, if carefully done, makes them more tender, yet preserves their natural colours and flavours. Certainly, cooking individual foods and mixtures enables man to have a wider variety of food on his dinner table. Heating, however, especially in the presence of large amounts of water, can cause destruction of vitamin C, thiamine, and solubility losses of valuable minerals.

Heating has an even more important function than merely enhancing palatability characteristics. By heating food to either boiling temperature of 100°C or higher to 116°C, harmful microorganisms and parasites that are natural contaminants of food are destroyed. Thus, *Staphylococcus* and *Salmonella* are destroyed by boiling, while *Clostridium botulinum* must be exposed to temperatures of 116° (attained under pressure) if heat resistant spores are to be eliminated from the product. Another example is *Trichinella*, a small helminth (parasitic worm) found in raw or uncooked pork. If consumed by humans, the worms migrate to human flesh, causing serious illness. But when pork is cooked to at least 58.5°C, the parasites are killed. Numerous protozoan and other worm parasites may cause human illness if people eat uncooked vegetables and fruits from gardens fertilized with human excreta. Although it is logical to associate such problems with primitive agriculture, they are also of concern today in some areas where organic gardening is not carefully practiced.

Except for grains and sugars, most foods eaten by man are perishable. They deteriorate in palatability and become spoiled when stored for long periods. Surplus animal and crop harvests, however, can be saved for future use if appropriate methods of preservation are used.

The major ways of preserving foods are canning, freezing, drying, salting and smoking. With all methods the aim is to kill or restrict the growth of harmful microorganisms and to slow or inactivate enzymes that cause undesirable changes in palatability. To further protect the preserved food while it is stored for long periods of time, it is placed either in metal cans, glass jars, air-tight paper or plastic containers.

While in many parts of the world, family groups continue to raise and preserve a large portion of their food for use throughout the year, in countries of the western world consumers rely heavily on both fresh and commercially processed foods purchased in nearby supermarkets.

Canning

Ever since Louis Pasteur proved that microorganisms, invisible to the eye, caused food to putrefy and that this putrefaction was not spontaneous decomposition, various methods of heating foods to temperatures high enough to kill harmful microorganisms have been employed. The basic process in canning foods is to heat the food to boiling or higher, pack and completely seal it in sterilized containers. The precise processing temperatures and times are dependent upon the acidity of the particular foodstuffs being processed. Foods with a more neutral pH (4.5 upward) require the high heat of pressure canners to ensure safe processing. Density of the foodstuff as well as size and shape of container also influence processing times.

The average energy input for canning vegetables and fruits is about 575 kcal kg^{-1} food (Table 10.1). This figure represents only the energy expended in actual processing by heat, and does not include the energy input required for making the container. (Packaging is discussed later in this chapter.)

Freezing

In freezing, many of the desirable qualities of the fresh food are retained for relatively long periods of time. The temperatures employed, $-18°C$, retard or prevent the growth of harmful microorganisms. Their growth is also inhibited by lack of water, which is frozen and hence not available to the microorganisms.

Fruits can be frozen as a dry pack with added dry sugar or in a syrup. Vegetables must be blanched (boiled or steamed a short time) prior to freezing to inactivate plant enzymes that cause deterioration of natural flavours and colours.

Table 10.1   Energy inputs for processing various products (after Casper, 1977).

Product	kcal kg^{-1}	Remarks
Beet sugar	5660	Assumed 17 % sugar in beets
Cane sugar	3370	Assumed 20 % sugar in cane
Fruit and vegetables (canned)	575	
Fruit and vegetables (frozen)	1815	
Flour	484	Includes blending of flour
Baked goods	1485	
Breakfast cereals	15 675	
Meat	1206	
Milk	354	
Dehydrated foods	3542	
Fish (frozen)	1815	
Ice cream	880	
Chocolate	18 591	
Coffee	18 948	Instant coffee
Soft drinks	1425	Per litre
Wine, brandy, spirits	830	Per litre
Pet food	828	
Ice production	151	

The energy inputs for freezing vegetables and fruits are significantly greater than for canning, averaging 1815 kcal kg^{-1} of food frozen compared with only 575 kcal kg^{-1} for canning (Table 10.1). This is because the canning process requires only heating, while freezing may involve brief heating, cooling, and then actual freezing.

Furthermore, canned foods can be stored at room temperature (actually slightly cooler is recommended), whereas frozen food must be kept in freezers at temperatures of $-18°C$ or lower. Maintaining such a low temperature requires about 265 kcal kg^{-1} per month of storage (USBC, 1975). Since frozen foods are usually stored 3–6 months, this energy cost must be added to the freezing cost, making the total energy input much greater than that for canning. However, the moisture-resistant plastic and paper containers for frozen foods require less energy to manufacture than the metal cans and glass jars used for canned food.

Salting

Fish, pork and other meats have been preserved by salting for over 3000 years (Jensen, 1949). This food processing method is not employed as widely today as it has been in the past, perhaps because other methods make possible the preservation of a wider variety of foods.

The principle of using salt (NaCl) for preserving fish and meats is to dehydrate the meat and, more importantly, to increase the osmotic pressure to a level where the growth of microorganisms, insects and other organisms is prevented.

Like sun-drying of foods in warm, sunny climates, salting requires a relatively small input of energy. Usually about 1 kg of salt is added per 4 kg of fish or meat that is to be salted and dried (Hertzberg *et al.*, 1973). The method requires an estimated 23 kcal kg^{-1} of fish or meat preserved (90 kcal of fossil energy is required to produce 1 kg of salt (Rawitscher and Mayer, 1977)).

The salted product can be stored by hanging in a cool/dry area or placing in an appropriate container. The total energy input of 23 kcal kg^{-1} is significantly lower than that required for freezing fish or meat.

Before the salted fish or meat can be eaten, the salt must be removed by soaking and rinsing the food many times with fresh water. Then the fish or meat is usually cooked, but even after the soaking and the rinsing there is usually a sufficient salt residue to give the fish or meat a noticeably salty taste.

Drying

Drying grains, meats, legumes and fruits by reducing the moisture level to 13 % or lower prevents the growth of harmful microorganisms and lessens chances for infestations by insects. Sunlight is an effective source of energy for drying that has been used for centuries and is still used today, especially for such crops as raisins and legumes. Sunlight as an energy source has the distinct advantage of being a continuous, unlimited source and generally costs little to use.

When not accomplished by the slow sun-drying method, drying becomes energy intensive because the removal of water requires large inputs of energy. In drying grains, for instance, the removal of one litre of water requires an average energy input of 3600 kcal (Leach, 1976). However, by using some of the most efficient technology available, Leach (1976) reports that it is possible to remove a litre of water from grain with an input of only 1107 kcal.

In investigating the drying of corn in the United States, Pimentel *et al.* (1973) reported an energy input of 1520 kcal per litre of water removed from corn; put another way, 1520 kcal are expended to reduce the moisture level of 7.4 kg of field-harvested corn from 26.5 % to 13 %. The average energy input used to dehydrate foods is 3542 kcal kg^{-1} of dehydrated food produced (Table 10.1). Thus the energy input for drying approximately equals the food energy contained in 1 kg of many typical grains (about 3400 kcal).

All these calculated energy inputs for removing moisture from foods are higher than the theoretical values for evaporating moisture. For example, the evaporation of one litre of water from an open container theoretically should require as little as a 620 kcal input (HCP, 1974). The reason that, in practice, 2–6 times more energy is generally required is because the water in the food is not as accessible as it is in an open dish. Instead, water must be removed from inside the cells of vegetables, fruits or meat. In other words, barriers must be overcome in order to remove the water from food and this requires extra energy.

In freeze-drying, a recently developed method of drying, the food is first frozen and then dried under high vacuum. This makes possible the attainment of a moisture content much lower than 13 %; the resultant food is exceptionally light and can be stored at room temperature. However, this process is even more energy intensive than regular drying, because energy is used both for freezing and drying.

Smoking

Smoking like drying, is a method of preservation that had its beginnings in primitive societies, yet is used today. Fish, meats and grains are the major foods preserved by this method. Basically, smoking preserves food in two ways. First, the heat of smoking dries or dehydrates the food, and second, the various tars, phenols, and other chemicals in the smoke are toxic to both microorganisms and insects.

In many developing countries, grains to be used by the farm family are hung from the ceiling of the kitchen area of the house where the smoke and heat from the open kitchen fire both dry and 'smoke' the stored grain. Insect and microorganism growth is minimized by this simple processing and storage method.

To smoke thin strips of a 1 kg fish, about 1 kg of hardwood such as hickory is used. Adding sand to the hardwood chips keeps it smouldering and smoking to process the fish or meat. The energy input for smoked fish is estimated to be about 4500 kcal kg^{-1}, with most of the energy coming from the wood chips burned in the smoking process.

Various processed and prepared foods

The energy inputs for preserved, processed and home-prepared foods are substantial. For example, in an analysis of the energy inputs of the production of a 1 kg loaf of white bread in the United Kingdom, Leach (1976) reported that 77 % of the 3795 kcal total energy used to produce the bread (including marketing costs) is used in processing, with 13 % for milling and 64 % for baking.

An analysis of U.S. technology shows that producing a 1 kg loaf of white bread requires an input of 7345 kcal, substantially greater than that for the United Kingdom. The milling and baking account for only 27 % of the total energy input compared with 77 % in Leach's analysis (Fig. 10.1). Of the 27 %, 7 % is for milling and 20 % for baking. Although 27 % for processing seems high, it is appreciably lower than the input for wheat production, which is 45 % of the total energy input. Hence, the major energy input for the white bread produced in the United States is expended for wheat grain production (Fig. 10.1).

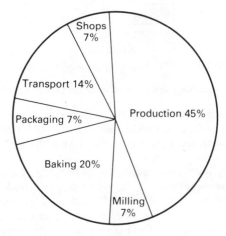

Fig. 10.1 Percentages of total inputs of 7345 kcal for the production, milling, baking, transport and shopping for a 1 kg loaf of bread.

The energy inputs to produce a 455 g can of sweet corn differ greatly from those expended for a loaf of white bread. For corn, the energy for production amounts to only a little more than 10 % of the total energy used to produce, process and market a can of sweet corn (Fig. 10.2). Most of the energy input of 1268 kcal is for processing because of the energy used in the production of the steel can. Specifically, the heat-processing of the corn requires only 262 kcal, but the production of the can requires about 1006 kcal.

The other large input that must be included in energy accounting for a given food is the energy expended by the consumer shopping for the food. In the United States, food shopping usually requires the use of a 1000 to 3000 kg automobile. Based on an allocation of the weight of the corn and the other groceries brought home from the supermarket, about 311 kcal are expended just to transport a 455 g can of corn home from the store. This is about 3/4 the amount of energy expended for producing the corn alone. Energy

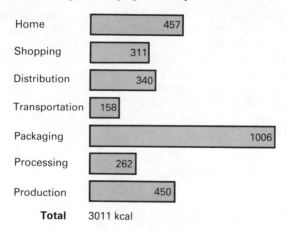

Fig. 10.2 Energy inputs for a 455 g can of sweet corn (= 375 kcal).

expended in home preparation amounts to 457 kcal or about 12 % of the total and includes cooking the corn and using an electric dishwasher to clean the pots, pans, plates and other utensils that are used.

All the energy inputs for producing, processing, packaging, transporting, and home-preparing a 455 g can of corn total 3011 kcal (Fig. 10.2). Contrast that with the 375 kcal of food energy provided by the corn. Hence, about 9 kcal of fossil energy are necessary to supply 1 kcal of sweet corn food energy at the dinner table.

The pattern of energy inputs for beef differs greatly from that for sweet corn (Fig. 10.3). Although 140 g of beef also provides about 375 kcal of food energy, about 29 000 kcal of fossil energy are expended just in the production of this amount of beef (Fig. 10.3). In other words, beef production requires about 6.5 times more energy per kcal of food energy produced than does sweet corn. The other energy inputs for beef production, such as transportation etc., are all relatively small compared to the production inputs. The prime reason being that large quantities of grain are fed to beef animals in U.S. production.

Energy accounting of the U.S. food system is complicated by the fact that most of the corn and other cereal grains suitable for human consumption are fed to livestock. Of the estimated 1300 kg grain produced per capita per year in the United States, only about 110 kg are consumed directly by humans (USDA, 1976b).

The energy inputs for processing several other food products are presented in Table 10.1. The relatively large inputs for processing of 1 kg of sugar, e.g. 3380 kcal for cane sugar and 5660 kcal for beet sugar, are due primarily to the energy used for the removal of water

Home	▍141
Shopping	▍96
Distribution	▍105
Transportation	▍50
Packaging	▍50
Processing	▍55
Production	██████████████████ 29 000
Total	29 497 kcal

Fig. 10.3 Energy inputs to supply 140 g beef (= 375 kcal) to the table.

by evaporation. As indicated earlier in this section, the evaporation of water is an energy-intensive technology. Thus, 1 kg of crystalline sugar, which has a food energy value of 3850 kcal, requires almost that much in energy inputs to process.

Breakfast cereals are also energy intensive to process and prepare. On the average, these require about 15 675 kcal kg^{-1} of cereal produced (Table 10.1). The energy inputs include those required for grinding, milling, wetting, drying and baking of the cereals. Other technologies, like extrusion processes, are sometimes used and these also require relatively large inputs of energy. Although 15 675 kcal are used in the production of 1 kg of breakfast cereal, this amount of cereal contains only about 3600 kcal of food energy.

Both chocolate and coffee concentrates are examples of energy-intensive food-processing techniques because of the energy used in roasting, grinding, wetting and drying the product. Processing of 1 kg of chocolate or coffee is reported to require more than 18 000 kcal kg^{-1} (Table 10.1).

The energy inputs for soft drink processing are high because of the pressurized systems that are employed to incorporate carbon dioxide (Table 10.1). A total of 1425 kcal are required per litre of soft drink produced. Note how much less energy is required in the processing of milk (354 kcal per litre).

Packages for Foods

In general, processed foods must be stored in some type of container. For instance, 455 g of frozen vegetable is usually placed in a small paper box that requires an expenditure of approximately 722 kcal of energy to make (Table 10.2).

Table 10.2 Energy required to produce various food packages (after Berry and Makino, 1974).

Package	kcal
Wooden berry basket	69
Styrofoam tray (size 6)	215
Moulded paper tray (size 6)	384
Polyethylene pouch (16 oz) or (455 g)	559*
Steel can, aluminum top (12 oz)	568
Small paper set-up box	722
Steel can, steel top (16 oz)	1006
Glass jar (16 oz)	1023
Coca Cola bottle, non-returnable (16 oz)	1471
Aluminum TV dinner container	1496
Aluminum can, pop-top (12 oz)	1643
Plastic milk container, disposable (1/2 gal)	2159
Coca Cola bottle, returnable (16 oz)	2451
Polyethylene bottle (1 qt)	2494
Polypropylene bottle (1 qt)	2752
Glass milk container returnable (1/2 gal)	4455

* Calculated from data of Berry and Makino.

In contrast, a like quantity (455 g) of a canned vegetable like corn is placed in a steel can that requires 1006 kcal to make (Table 10.2). If the vegetables were packed in a glass jar, the energy input for the container would be 1023 kcal or about the same as that used to produce a steel can (Table 10.2).

Thus, just to process 455 g of corn and place it into a steel can requires a total input of about 1270 kcal of energy (Fig. 10.2). This is less than the about 1550 kcal expended in freezing 455 g of vegetable and placing it in a cardboard box. But as mentioned, the frozen foods have an added energy cost since the foods must be stored at $0°$ C or lower in a freezer that requires about 265 kcal kg^{-1} per month to operate.

Although there is little difference between the energy inputs required for the production of steel cans and glass jars, there is a significant increase in the energy inputs for producing aluminum soft drink cans. A 355 ml steel can for soft drinks requires an input of about 570 kcal; the same size aluminum can requires 1643 kcal, nearly three times as much energy for production (Table 10.2). Note that the soft drink that is placed in a 355 ml can contains about 150 kcal food energy in the form of sugar, equivalent to about 10 % of the energy that was expended in the production of the aluminum can. Or a more extreme illustration is the high energy cost of an aluminum can made to contain a diet soft drink that has only 1 kcal per can.

Another example of the large energy input in food containers is the aluminum food trays commonly used to hold frozen TV dinners. An average tray requires about 1500 kcal to make (Table 10.2). The amount of energy expended for the tray is often greater than the food energy that is in the food itself, which usually ranges from 800 to 1000 kcal.

In addition, the diverse containers that are used to display fruits, vegetables, and meats in grocery stores all require energy for production. Energy expenditures range from about 70 kcal for wood berry baskets to 380 kcal for a moulded paper tray (Table 10.2).

Because of increased concern about the desirability of recycling beverage containers, the energy inputs of recycling milk and beverage bottles has been analyzed. A disposable plastic half-gallon milk container requires 2160 kcal for production, whereas a half-gallon glass container requires 4445 kcal (Table 10.2). With twice as much energy 'invested' in the glass container, two uses of the returnable glass container are required to equal the initial energy input for the plastic container. Actually, more than two uses of the returnable glass bottles would be required for an energy saving to be realized. Then, too, added energy is expended to collect, transport, sort and clean the re-useable glass container.

As with milk containers, returnable glass beverage bottles require more energy for production than do non-returnable bottles (Table 10.2). A 16 oz returnable soft drink bottle requires about 2450 kcal for production, compared to about 1470 kcal for the same size non-returnable bottle. Again, two uses of the returnable bottle would more than offset the production input. However, as with milk containers, the energy costs of collecting, transporting and cleaning the returnable bottles must be examined relative to the whole system. Considering only the energy expended in the production of the bottle does not give a complete picture of the energy cost involved. Of course other considerations such as environmental pollution caused by non-returnable containers must be weighed along with energy expenditure before community policies can be decided upon.

Cooking and Preparing Foods

Foods for human consumption are often cooked or reheated in the home and this requires an expenditure of more energy.

In the United States, an estimated 9025 kcal of fossil energy are used per person per day just for home refrigeration and heating of food (USBC, 1975). This averages out to an estimated 4649 kcal kg^{-1} of food prepared. These estimates are based on the following data and assumptions: (1) each residential customer uses an average of 7900 kWh per year (USBC, 1975); (2) 40 % of this energy is expended for food preparation, including refrigeration (USBC, 1975); (3) the efficiency of producing electricity from fossil fuel is calculated to be 33 %; (4) the average number of persons per home is 2.5 and each person consumes an average of 705 kg (1550 lbs) of food per year (USDA, 1976b).

Depending on the food, the fuel used, the material of the cooking containers, method of preparation and stove used, the energy input varies considerably. There appears to be little difference between the energy expended for baking, boiling or broiling foods. This assumes that the exposure of the food to heat is optimal and that the cooking utensils allow for efficient heat transfer to the food itself. Note that not only the shape and materials used in construction of the cooking utensil will affect the transfer of heat but the colour also influences cooking efficiency. A shiny aluminum pan reflects much heat and is therefore less efficient than one with a dark, dull surface or one made from glass. Furthermore, the nature of the food itself, fluid, viscous or dense, will either slow or speed heat transfer, increasing or decreasing the amount of energy used in a particular process. Due to these variables it is difficult to calculate precise energy expenditures, but it is important to acknowledge that they are part of energy accounting.

The transfer of heat from stoves to foods is relatively inefficient. For example, an electric stove is 75 % efficient and a gas stove 37 % efficient in transferring heat from the burner to the food that is being cooked (SRI, 1972).

Nevertheless, the gas stove is much more efficient overall than the electric stove for use in cooking because the production and transport of gas to the home uses only about 10 % of the energy potential of gas. Thus the production and transport of gas energy is 90 % efficient. Multiplying this 90 % efficiency by the 37 % efficiency of transfer of heat to the item cooked yields a 33 % overall efficiency for gas cooking.

For electricity the picture is much more complex. First, mining and transporting the coal reduces the energy potential of the coal by 8 %. This means that 92 % of the initial energy potential of the coal is available at the power plant for subsequent electric power generation. Let us assume that the power plant is 33 % efficient in converting coal to electricity and that the transmission of the electricity to the home is 92 % efficient. Also, assume that the transmission of heat from electric stove to food is, at best, 75 % efficient. Then taking into account the successive losses in potential energy that occur throughout the entire process $(100 \times 0.92 \times 0.33 \times 0.92 \times 0.75)$, the overall efficiency rate for electricity is only 21 %. This means that cooking by electricity is only about 2/3rds (21 % vs 33 %) as efficient as gas. Hydro-electric power is more efficient than electric power derived from coal because heat (steam) production is not necessary with hydro-electric power.

Less efficient than either electricity or gas is cooking with charcoal or wood over an open hearth, as is often done in developing nations. Employing an open fire to heat food is 8–10 % efficient in transmitting heat to the food (Stanford, 1977). This, then, is both an inefficient and costly use of fuel. Using a simple wood-burning stove would increase the energy efficiency to 20–25 % and thereby reduce the fuel cost.

The inefficiency of cooking food over an open wood fire stove can easily be demonstrated. If 600 kcal are required to cook 1 kg of food, then using an open wood fire would require 6000 kcal of energy from wood at an efficiency rate of 10 % for cooking. The food itself, if a grain like rice, would contain 3500 kcal of food energy. Hence, nearly twice as much energy would be used to cook the food than is actually present in the food itself.

Cooking food in developing nations requires nearly 2/3 of the total energy expended in the food system while production requires about 1/3 of the total (Table 10.3). Almost all of the energy used for cooking comes from renewable energy sources, primarily firewood and charcoal, dung and crop residues, which are burned over the open hearth.

Table 10.3 Model of annual per capita use of energy in the food system of rural population in developing countries (from Pimentel, 1974; Pimentel, 1976; Pimentel and Beyer, 1976; RSAS, 1976; Revelle, 1976; Ernst, 1978).

	Fossil energy (kcal)	Renewable energy (kcal)	Total
Production	130 000	490 000	620 000
Processing	15 000	20 000	35 000
Storage	5000	20 000	25 000
Transport	30 000	20 000	50 000
Preparation	20 000	1 250 000	1 270 000
Total	200 000	1 800 000	2 000 000

Special mention should be made of charcoal, which is commonly used for cooking, and how it compares with wood as a fuel. True, cooking over an open charcoal fire is similar to using wood or about 10 % efficient in the transfer of heat energy to the food. However, charcoal production is extremely energy-intensive.

The misleading factor about charcoal is its apparently high energy content, for it contains 7100 kcal kg^{-1} of energy when burned.

However, this fact has to be placed in perspective. A total of 28 400 kcal of hardwood has to be processed to obtain the 7100 kcal of charcoal, a 25 % efficiency in the conversion of hardwood calories into charcoal calories. Thus, the use of charcoal for heating food over an open fire results in an overall efficiency in energy transfer of only 2.5 % (100 ×0.25 ×0.10). Indeed this is an extremely inefficient and costly way to transfer energy. In addition, if we are concerned about conserving forest and firewood supplies and making the most efficient use of them, encouraging the use of charcoal for fuel defeats these aims (Eckholm, 1976). Certainly using charcoal in preference to wood is an ineffective way to conserve and use wisely the important renewable resources of our forests.

11 Transport of Agricultural Supplies and Food

Transport is an essential component of all food systems and especially those in industrialized nations like the United States. Such nations have both highly developed industrial complexes and intensive agricultural programs. Their agricultural production is characterized by food crops that are grown in specialized regions where agriculture is the most productive (e.g. corn (maize) belt of the United States). Industrial production sites are generally located near population centres and available power sources.

With agriculture and industry often located in widely separated regions, transport is essential for the use and exchange of all goods and materials. Thus, harvested crops have to be transported to the cities and towns where industry is located. Then supplies of machinery, fertilizers, pesticides, fuel and other goods have to be transported back to farms for continuing crop and livestock production.

Transportation in the food system is vastly more complex than just shipping food directly from the farm to an individual home. Most food crops after being processed and packaged are then transported to large wholesale distribution centres. From these centres the packaged foods are then shipped to retail stores located closer to the consumer. It is there the consumer selects, purchases and transports them home.

To clarify the energy expended in this vast network, the energy inputs in transporting goods to the farm, raw agricultural products to the processors, produce to wholesale-retail markets and, finally, food from the grocery to home will be analyzed.

Transport of Agricultural Supplies and Goods to the Farm

An estimated 160×10^6 ha of land is cultivated annually in the United States for crops (USDA, 1976a). The total quantity of goods and supplies transported to farms for use in agricultural production amounts to about 110×10^9 kg (USDA, 1976a). This means that, on the average, about 600 kg of needed goods and supplies must be transported to farms for each hectare cultivated. Available data indicate that about 60 % of the goods transported from factory to farm move by rail and the remaining 40 % by truck. The average distance these goods are transported is about 640 km (USDC, 1963).

The energy inputs to move goods by truck are estimated to be 0.83 kcal kg^{-1} km^{-1} (Table 11.1). This is based on the facts that trucks travel an estimated 3.6 km per litre of gasoline and transport an average of 3 600 kg of goods per truck (USBC, 1976).

The energy input to move goods by rail is estimated to be 0.12 kcal kg^{-1} km^{-1} (Table 11.1). Thus, rail transport requires about 1/7th of the energy expended in truck transport (Table 11.1).

Table 11.1   Energy inputs for transporting a kilogram one kilometre by various methods.

Transport	kcal kg^{-1} km^{-1}
Waterway	0.08[a]
Rail	0.12[a]
Truck	0.83[b]
Air	6.36[a]

(a) Hirst, 1972.
(b) USBC, 1976.

To calculate the energy input for transporting goods and supplies to the farm, we use the data of the USDC (1963) that 600 kg of goods and supplies are transported to each farm hectare; that 60 % of the goods is transported by rail and 40 % by truck; and that the average distance that the goods are transported is 640 km (USDC, 1963). The energy input for the 60 % transported by rail is about 26 960 kcal and for the 40 % transported by truck, 127 490 kcal. This makes a total energy input of 154 450 kcal to transport the 600 kg of goods for each crop hectare. Thus, 257 kcal energy is expended for transport of one kg of goods to the farm for use in agricultural production or 402 kcal $tonne^{-1}$ km^{-1}. Annually then, an estimated 26.4×10^{12} kcal is required to transport the total 110×10^9 kg goods and supplies needed on U.S. farms. This energy expenditure is the equivalent of 164×10^6 barrels of petroleum.

Transport of Food and Fibre Products from the Farm

Annually about 160×10^6 ha of cropland are harvested and an average of 3360 kg of crop products are harvested per hectare. This means an estimated 518×10^6 tonnes of farm produce comprised of food and fibre products are transported from the farm to various locations for eventual use.

As mentioned, the transport of food and related products in the United States is estimated to be about 60 % by truck and about 40 % by rail. Using the data in Table 11.1, the energy required to move 1 kg of food and fibre products is calculated to be approximately 0.50 kcal km^{-1}. If the average distance the goods are moved is 640 km (USDC, 1963), then the energy input per kg moved is 349 kcal.

The 349 kcal kg^{-1} transported is an average figure. Frequently much greater energy inputs are made for transporting food. For instance, consider the journey of a 0.5 kg head of lettuce that has an energy value of about 50 kcal. When this head of lettuce is transported by truck from California to New York, a distance of 4827 km, the energy expended is about 1800 kcal. This means that just for transport, about 36 kcal of energy are expended per kcal of food energy in the lettuce.

Even greater quantities of energy are used to transport strawberries from California to New York. Early in the spring, when strawberries are harvested in California, they are sometimes flown from California to New York. The energy used to air-transport 1 kg of strawberries, which has 354 kcal food energy, is calculated to be 30 700 kcal. This means approximately 87 kcal of fossil energy was spent per kcal of strawberry just to provide a distant New Yorker with fresh strawberries.

Data from the food processing industry generally confirms the average input of 349 kcal kg^{-1} to transport processed food to consumer market. For example, data from the milling and baking industry indicate that 495 kcal are expended to transport each kilogram of bakery goods produced to market (Casper, 1977). For fluid milk, the calculated inputs for collection and redistribution are about 381 kcal of fossil energy for each kilogram of milk produced (Casper, 1977).

Transport of Food from Grocery to Home

Annually in the United States more than half of the 2.4 tonnes of food and food products produced per person is fed to livestock; some is wasted in processing. Thus, the amount actually consumed per person is about 700 kg (USDA, 1976b).

To calculate the energy required to transport this 700 kg of food from the grocery store to the home, information is needed on family size, number of trips to grocery, distance and vehicle used.

With the average family, consisting of 2.5 people, the total annual amount of food transported home from the grocery is about 1550 kg. The number of trips made to the grocery store per week is 2.26 (Dietrich, 1975), and about 15 kg of food is transported home from the grocery on each shopping trip. The average distance between supermarket and home is estimated to be about 2.4 km, making a round trip of 4.8 km.

Over 90 % of grocery shopping in the United States is done using an automobile (Dietrich, 1975) that averages 6.3 km per litre of fuel (USBC, 1976). The input to move an automobile 1 km is calculated to be 1885 kcal, making the energy input for fuel for the round trip to the grocery 9048 kcal. In addition, a calculated 31 968 000 kcal of energy is required to construct a 1545 kg auto (Berry and Fels, 1973). If the auto travels 160 000 km during its total use, and requires an added energy expenditure of 10 % in repairs, then 1200 kcal must be added to the input for transporting 15 kg of food from the grocery. Therefore, the energy input for bringing groceries home from the market is 682 kcal kg^{-1} purchased.

This amounts to an expenditure of 310 kcal to transport a 455 g can of food home. If the can contained sweet corn, for instance, then 310 kcal fossil energy is used to transport 455 g of corn which contains only 375 kcal. The transportation process becomes even less energy efficient when foods contain even fewer calories per unit weight. Therefore because a 0.5 kg head of lettuce contains only about 50 kcal, transporting the lettuce home requires more than six times the food energy contained in the lettuce.

If the food were transported from the grocery store by bicycle, the energy input would be considerably smaller. Assuming that a bicycle travels at 20 km per hour and the operator burns 300 kcal per hour in operation, this works out to be approximately 15 kcal km^{-1} of bike travel. The 4.8 km round shopping trip would there-fore require 72 kcal, plus 1 kcal for construction and maintenance of the bicycle. Again assuming that 15 kg of groceries were trans-ported home each trip, about 2.2 kcal would be expended for the 455 g of canned sweet corn transported. Thus, transporting food from the grocery store by automobile requires the expenditure of 141 times as much energy as the same task would require using a bicycle. If the groceries were transported by walking, total energy input would be about 300 kcal or about 9 kcal for the 455 g can. This is about four times more energy expended in walking than bicycling.

12 Food, Energy and the Future of Our Society

Two thirds of the world population consumes primarily a vegetarian-type diet. In these areas about 182 kg grain products are consumed yearly per person. This grain is consumed directly and little food of animal origin is eaten. In contrast, the remaining 1/3rd of the world, including people living in industrial countries like the United States, consumes about 115 kg animal foods yearly per person (USDA, 1976a). To produce this amount of animal food in the United States about 605 kg of grain per person are raised and then fed to animals (USDA, 1976a).

One cannot help speculating how large the world supply of food would have to be if the 2/3rds who presently eat mainly grain products were to switch to a diet similar to that consumed in the United States. A more practical question may be whether man will be able to provide a nutritionally satisfactory diet for his numbers if, as projected, the world population escalates to about 6000 million by the year 2000.

The demand for food is dependent on and interrelated with many factors of the vast human social and ecological system. Fundamentally, this demand depends upon human population numbers and standard of living desired (Fig. 12.1). Food supplies are influenced by such factors as arable land, water, climate, fertilizer and fossil energy. Food supplies are also affected by public health, losses due to pests, availability of labour, environmental pollution and the lifestyle of the people.

Future Food Needs

Human population growth

The rapid growth of the world population has resulted in an increased need for food. FAO estimates that today nearly one half billion humans, approximately 15 % of the population of the developing countries, are seriously malnourished (UN, 1974).

For about a million years, the human population growth rate was slow, averaging only about 0.001 % per year. During that long

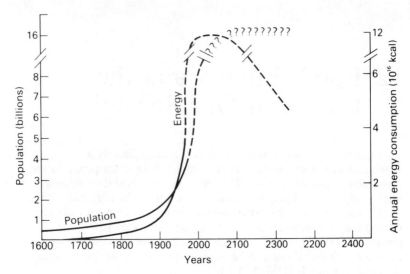

Fig. 12.1 Estimated world population numbers (——) from 1600 to 1975 and projected numbers (– – – –) (?????) to the year 2250. Estimated fossil fuel consumption (——) from 1650 to 1975 and projected (– – – –) to the year 2250 (after Pimentel *et al.*, 1975).

period of time the world population numbered less than 10 million (Keyfitz, 1976). Growth in human population numbers began to escalate about 8–10 thousand years ago when agriculture was first initiated. Rapid population growth, however, actually started after 1700, when it accelerated to today's rate of nearly 2 % per year – 2000 times the historical rate of 0.001 % (NAS, 1975; Keyfitz, 1976). World population now stands at over 4000 million and is expanding at the rate of 200 000 persons per day, and unless unforeseen factors intervene, it will reach at least 6000 million by 2000 (NAS, 1971; UN, 1973; NAS, 1975). Stability and maximum population numbers are not expected to be reached until after the year 2100 when the world population is projected to attain a level of from 10 to 16 000 million (UN, 1973; NAS, 1975).

At this point it is relevant to consider seriously Malthus' biological law (1798). He stated his proposition as follows: 'I think I may fairly make two postulata; first, that food is necessary to the existence of man. Secondly, that the passion between the sexes is necessary and will remain nearly in its present state . . . Assuming then my postulata as granted, I say, that the power of population is definitely greater than the power of the earth to produce substance for man.' In the face of present reality, Malthus may be proven correct. Historical evidence documents many periods of time when certain human populations increased above the level their food supply could sustain, and severe regional famines occurred. None of these were of the magnitude of the catastrophic famine projected for the future (Walford, 1878; Morison, 1911; Mallory, 1928; Spengler, 1968).

Perhaps Bertrand Russell (1961) best expressed the biological law related to population growth when he wrote: 'Every living thing is a sort of imperialist seeking to transform as much as possible of its environment into itself and its seed.' This law of natural populations suggests that species populations will increase until food or other resources become limiting. Our hope is that man has the wisdom to limit his numbers and to ensure a quality life, which provides one with adequate food and shelter.

Population health

Rapid growth in the world population coincided with the exponential use of fossil fuels (Fig. 12.1). This energy was used for public health and disease control programs, and to increase food production for the ever-growing world population. The control of typhoid disease, for example, necessitated improving water facilities, a process that required large energy expenditures (Audy, 1964). The program for eradicating malaria-carrying mosquitoes required applying DDT and other insecticides. Producing these insecticides used substantial quantities of energy (Audy, 1964).

Reducing death rates by effective disease control has been followed by substantial increases in population growth rates. For example, in Ceylon, after spraying with DDT the death rate fell from 20 in 1946 to 14 per thousand in 1947 (PEP, 1955) and concurrently population growth rates increased. A similar dramatic reduction in death rate occurred after DDT was used on the island of Mauritius, where death rates fell from 27 to 15 per thousand in one year and population growth rates increased from about 5 to 35 per thousand (Fig. 12.2).

Recent historical evidence documents similar occurrences in nations where public health technology and medical supplies have significantly reduced death rates (Corsa and Oakley, 1971). The effective control of human diseases, coupled with increased food production, has contributed significantly to rapid population growth (NAS, 1971). Unfortunately, the immediate increase in family size and explosive population increase in cities, towns, and villages all too often overwhelms the existing social and food production systems (NAS, 1971).

The mere presence of some chronic diseases also increases the need for food supplies. For example, when a person is ill with

Fig. 12.2 Population growth rate on Mauritius from 1920 to 1970. Note from 1920 to 1945 the growth rate was about 5 per thousand whereas after malaria control in 1945 the growth rate exploded to about 35 per thousand and has since very slowly declined (PEP, 1955; UN, 1957–1971). After 25 years the rate of increase is still nearly 4 times the 1920–45 level.

diarrhoea, malaria, or is infested with a parasite like hookworms, anywhere from 5 to 20 % of the individual's energy intake goes to offset the illness. Specifically with malaria, hookworms and amoebic dysentary, feeding by the parasites removes blood and nutrients and also reduces the ability of the individual to make effective use of his food. This type of situation can be considered as one that causes food losses.

Food losses

Significant quantities of our food supply are lost because of various pests such as insects, pathogens, weeds, birds and rodents. At present, world crop losses due to pest infestations are estimated to be about 35 % (Cramer, 1967; Pimentel, 1977). These losses include destruction by insects (13 %), pathogens (12 %), weeds (9 %), and mammals and birds (1 %). Although mammal and bird losses are more severe in the tropics and subtropics than in the temperate regions, these losses are low compared to those attributed to insects, pathogens and weeds.

In addition, available evidence tends to suggest that the green revolution technology has intensified losses to pests (Pradhan, 1971; I. Oka (1975) personal communication). The new high-yield varieties have exhibited a relatively high susceptibility to pests compared with the formerly planted varieties. In the past, farmers saved seeds from individual plants that survived and yielded best under native cultural conditions and planted them in subsequent seasons. These genotypes naturally contained several alleles that were resistant to insects and pathogens, as well as competitive with weeds (I. Oka (1975) personal communication). In this way farmers were developing genotypes that grew best in their localities.

The newly developed grain varieties have more genetic uniformity and this can become a distinct disadvantage when the variety is planted over large areas in a new environment. This is because an ideal ecological environment is provided for pathogens to evolve to a highly destructive level (Frankel, 1971; I. Oka (1975) personal communication). Concurrently, programs have been developed for multiple cropping in an effort to increase food supplies from limited land resources. The result of this type of continuous crop culture has been increased pest outbreaks (Pathak, 1975). Increased losses of crop due to pest damage mean a lower crop yield and less food.

All losses do not occur during the growing season as indicated by substantial post-harvest losses. These are estimated to range from an estimated 9 % in the United States (USDA, 1965) to a high of 20 % in some developing nations, especially those located in the tropics. The major pests that destroy harvested foods are micro-organisms, insects and rodents.

When post-harvest losses are added to pre-harvest losses, total food losses due to pests rise to an estimated 48 %. Thus, the pests are consuming and/or destroying nearly 1/2 of the potential world food supply. Certainly it becomes quite clear that we cannot afford a loss of such magnitude when we face an increasing need for food to feed the growing world population.

Strategies for Meeting Food Needs

Sufficient calories, proteins, and certain essential vitamins and minerals must be provided man through his food if he is to achieve his genetic potential and achieve a full satisfying life. Our analyses have centred on production of protein foods and protein needs because their response to various environmental conditions is representative of all foods that contribute to the food supply.

At present, about 122×10^6 tonnes of plant/animal protein are produced annually worldwide. If evenly divided, this would provide about 84 g of protein per person per day. Of this total amount, animal protein (meat, milk, eggs, etc.) accounts for 25 %, or about 30×10^6 tonnes (Table 6.1). Livestock in the world today number about 1000×10^6 cattle, 1000×10^6 sheep, 350×10^6 goats, 100×10^6 buffalo, 11×10^6 camels, 550×10^6 pigs, 64×10^6 horses, 15×10^6 mules and 40×10^6 asses (Byerly, 1966). These 3.1×10^9 livestock graze an average of 1.6 ha per head. This estimate includes about 3×10^9 ha of available pasture and range, plus about 2×10^9 ha of forest and other suitable grazing land.

To increase production of animal protein, ways have to be found to make it more efficient than it has been in the past. Some estimates suggest that the fish harvest might be increased from 66×10^6 tonnes to 100×10^6 (Institute of Ecology, 1972). This is probably an over optimistic projection, because serious over-fishing problems already exist (Brown *et al.*, 1976) and, in fact, world fish catches have declined during the past few years (see Fig. 9.1). In addition, fish production is energy intensive; this has been and will continue to be a constraint on its expansion.

Livestock production could be improved if over-grazing were reduced and more productive pasture plant species were developed and cultured. Applications of limited amounts of fertilizers would increase yields of forage. The annual supply of animal protein could conceivably be increased from the present 33×10^6 tonnes to about 43×10^6 tonnes by the year 2000 (Table 6.1). This increase, however, would not be sufficient to maintain the present available plant/animal protein intake of 84 g per person per day for the entire world population.

An estimated 66% increase in legume production, a 100% increase in other vegetables, and a 75% increase in cereal production would enable the 1975 level of protein intake to be maintained for the projected 6–7 billion people expected to inhabit the world by 2000 A.D. Based on our analyses, these large increases in plant protein production are technically feasible during the next 25 years.

Perhaps an easier way to increase the supplies of protein and other foods is for man to become more vegetarian in his eating habits. Currently, an estimated 51×10^6 tonnes of plant protein suitable for man is fed annually to the world's livestock (Table 6.1). This represents 42% added protein that would be available to the world population if a change to vegetarianism were made in the future.

67×10^6 tonnes of protein suitable for man would have to be fed to livestock in the year 2000 to provide present levels of protein intake. If this were used directly for human consumption, significant reductions in the projected increases for cereal, legume, and vegetable protein could be made (see alternative plan for year 2000 in Table 6.1). Assuming that improved management of livestock pasture and rangeland yielded an additional 25×10^6 tonnes of livestock protein, then the increases needed in the following crops would be: cereals, 41%; legumes, 20%; and other plant proteins, 50%. Increased yields in plant crop production are more easily achieved than increases in animal production (Table 6.1).

Nevertheless, just as livestock production is vital to man today, it will be important to him in the future. Cattle, sheep and goats will continue to be of value because they convert grasses and shrubs on pastures and rangeland into food suitable for man. Without them man cannot make use of this type of vegetation.

Energy Needs in Food Production

Although in past decades man did not have to concern himself about fossil fuel supplies, this situation has changed. An estimated 16.5 % of the fossil energy used in the United States is spent in our food system (FEA, 1975). This 16.5 % may not seem either large or important when considered as a portion of the total U.S. energy expenditure, but compared to that of other nations, it is a large energy expenditure. For example, 16.5 % of the fossil fuel used in the United States actually amounts to 0.026 barrels of petroleum per capita per day, and is about twice the total daily per capita fossil fuel used in all of the developing nations (Fig. 1.2).

The following analysis may help clarify the relationships of fossil fuel supplies to production of food supplies. The total energy used annually in the United States for food production, processing, distribution and preparation amounts to about 1400 litres of oil per capita. Using the U.S. agricultural technology to feed the present world population of 4000 million, a high protein diet for one year would require an equivalent of 5760×10^9 litres of fuel annually.

Another way to explore the dependency of food production on fossil energy expenditure is to calculate how long it would take to deplete the known world reserve of petroleum if a high protein/calorie diet, produced using U.S. agricultural technologies, were fed to the entire world population. The known reserves have been estimated to be 86912×10^9 litres (Jiler, 1972) so if we assume that 75 % of the raw petroleum can be converted to fuel (Jiler, 1972) this would equal a useable reserve of 66053×10^9 litres. Assuming petroleum were the only source of energy for food production, and all known petroleum reserves were used solely for food production, the reserve would last a mere 11 years. This estimate is based on producing a food supply for a population of 4000 million.

But how can we balance food supply and energy expenditures against a growing world population? Even a doubling of the food supply during the next 25 years will not offset the serious conditions of malnourishment that 500 million humans presently endure. To double food supplies in this period would require a three-to-four-fold increase in the total quantity of energy that goes into food production. The reason for the large energy input per increment increase in food is due to the declining crop yield increment per energy input such as fertilizers (Fig. 12.3).

One practical way to increase food supplies with minimal fossil energy inputs is for the world population as a whole to consume more plant foods. This diet modification would reduce the energy expenditures and also increase food supplies because less human foods would be fed to livestock. With livestock, roughly 20 calories of increased energy is needed to obtain an additional calorie of production over a current yield of 1 calorie.

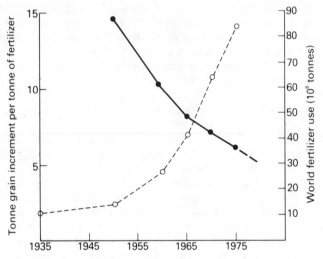

Fig. 12.3 Declining grain yield increment per fertilizer input (———) (Brown, 1978c) and world fertilizer use (.....) in metric tonnes.

Land Constraints

To feed a population of over 4000 million a U.S. high protein-calorie diet, produced with U.S. agricultural technology, would require large areas of arable land. This is also true if only plant production is to be increased. Thus it is important to know how much arable land is available to be used.

In the United States, about 160×10^6 ha are planted for crops (USDA, 1976a). With about 215 million people in the United States, this averages out to 0.77 ha per capita planted to crops. However, the arable land per person is reduced to about 0.62 ha because 20% of our crop yield is exported.

World arable land resources are estimated to be about 1.5×10^9 ha. Based on the present 4000 million world population, the available arable land amounts to only 0.38 ha per capita. Therefore, if at least 0.62 ha per capita is needed to produce a U.S.-type diet, there is not sufficient arable land, even assuming that energy resources and other technology were also available, to feed the world a U.S. diet.

Of course it may be possible to bring some poor land into production. Best estimates are that cropland resources might be expanded by about 15% to 2×10^9 ha without great cost and effort (NAS, 1977). In addition, marginal lands like marshlands could be drained or some arid land irrigated, increasing the potential about 25% or 3.4×10^9 ha (Kovda, 1971; NAS, 1977; Buringh *et al.*, 1975). This would, however, necessitate large energy and technological inputs. At a maximum population of 16 000 million, land satisfactory for cultivation per capita would only be 0.2 ha. On a worldwide basis, it is quite obvious that land suitable for cultivation is a serious constraint on food production.

This 0.2 ha per capita assumes that no degradation of arable land will occur. Unfortunately, even now our precious arable land is being lost and/or degraded at an alarming rate. For example, in the United States from 1945 to 1970, over 29×10^6 ha of land were lost to highways and urbanization. About half of this had been productive cropland (USDA, 1971a and 1974c) and represents an irreversible loss of land.

Erosion by wind and water seriously reduces the productivity of land. In the United States, the rate of soil erosion per hectare is estimated at 27 tonnes annually (Wadleigh, 1968; Hargrove, 1972). At this rate an estimated 80×10^6 ha already has been either totally ruined for crop production or has been so seriously eroded that it is only marginally suitable for production (USNRB, 1935; Bennett, 1939; Pimentel *et al.*, 1976). This relatively high rate of soil erosion has resulted in the loss of at least 1/3rd of topsoil from U.S. cropland in use today (Handler, 1970). Fortunately, up to the present time, the reduced productivity of U.S. cropland due to soil erosion has been offset by increased fertilizers and other fossil energy inputs (Hargrove, 1972). Specifically about 47 litres of fuel equivalents per hectare per year are being expended to offset the deterioration caused by erosion (Pimentel *et al.*, 1976). In developing countries, the rate at which cropland has eroded is nearly twice as great as it is in the United States (Ingraham, 1975), and resources to offset this loss have not been readily available in these areas. Thus, based on what we presently know, both the amount of arable land available for crop production and the amounts of extra energy needed to put poor land into production create serious constraints on expansion of crop production.

Water Constraints

Most crop plants use large quantities of water; most is supplied by rainfall. A hectare of corn, for example, requires from $6-12 \times 10^6$ litres (2–4 acre-feet) of water per growing season. In the United States, agricultural production uses about 96 % of the water that is consumed, whereas industry and urban areas, together, consume less than 4 % (NAS, 1974a).

If rainfall is insufficient, ways must be found to provide water and this is usually done by irrigation. Only about 14 % of the world's cultivated land is now irrigated (Buringh *et al.*, 1975). In arid lands, various sectors of the economy have conflicting demands for available water. That is, agriculture, urban population, industry and mining all require substantial amounts of this scarce resource. Indications are that changes in water allocation are inevitable, and that the proportion of water allocated to agriculture will decline. This is because the economic yields from agriculture per quantity of water used are far less than yields from either industry or mining (Gertel and Wollman, 1960).

Expansion of irrigation is further limited because it requires large amounts of energy. About 20.6×10^6 kcal of energy is needed to pump 12×10^6 litres of water from a depth of 30 m and sprinkler irrigate 1 ha of corn (Smerdon, 1974). This is more than three times the fossil energy inputs (6.6×10^6 kcal) usually expended to produce a hectare of corn employing U.S. technology. In addition, 13 % more energy is required both for supplying and maintaining the irrigation equipment. These figures do not include the environmental cost of salination of soil water or soil water logging problems that are often associated with irrigation.

In contrast to limited water supplies is the situation where too much water or rapid water runoff causes serious environmental problems. The removal of forests and other vegetation on slopes, in particular, encourages water runoff and often results in serious flood damage to crops and pasture (Beasley, 1972). In fact, losses due to 'flood water, sediment, and related water shed damage' (USDA, 1965) are estimated to be as high as $ 1300 million a year in the United States. Water runoff decreases crop yield per hectare by decreasing the amount of fertile soil, by washing out valuable soil constituents, and also washing out the crops themselves.

Climate

Climate has always determined both the suitability and availability of cropland for cultivation of crops. For this reason, changes in temperature and/or rainfall can be expected to influence future food supplies. These two considerations must be evaluated on different time scales. Within any given decade, there are likely to occur, as aberrations from the normal, irregularities in temperature and rainfall patterns that are capable of either improving crop yields or inflicting enormous damage to agricultural yields. In addition, there are long-term climatic trends that eventually will have major effects on agriculture.

An evaluation of long-term trends shows that the mean temperature of the northern hemisphere reached a maximum in about 1940. Since then, temperatures have declined about 0.1°C per decade (Bryson, 1974; Malone, 1974; Bryson and Wendland, 1975). Because a mere 0.6°C drop in temperature shortens a growing season by about two weeks (Malone, 1974), crop yields can be expected to be substantially reduced in marginal crop growing regions if the trend continues. For instance, in the U.S. corn belt, shortening the critical corn growing season by two weeks would result in a yield reduction of nearly 882 kg (34.6 bu) per hectare (H. Stockdale, Iowa State University, personal communication, 1975).

In addition to changes in temperature or rainfall, other environmental factors may influence food production. For example, the increased consumption of fossil energy by a growing industry and a rapidly expanding world population, may have an impact on climate and, in turn, an adverse impact on agriculture. The consumption of enormous quantities of fossil fuel, especially coal, is expected to significantly increase the carbon dioxide content and particulate matter (aerosols) of the atmosphere (Kellogg, 1975; Singer, 1975; Schneider, 1976). The precise impact these changes will have on the climate is not yet known. Any substantial increase, however, will probably result in major ecological changes that eventually will influence agricultural production.

The changes wrought by irregularities of climatic patterns call attention to the interdependency of nations and the importance of cooperative planning among all nations. The effects of such irregularities also emphasize the need for an international food reserve to offset years in which crop yields in the food producing regions of the world are unexpectedly low.

Environmental Pollution

The carbon dioxide and particulate matter released by the burning of fossil fuels is considered environmental pollution. Another type of environmental pollution directly associated with agriculture is the use of pesticides. Pesticides significantly reduce pest problems in agriculture and protect human health by eliminating disease-spreading pests. Pesticides, however, also are responsible for serious environmental and health problems. As an example of the latter, pesticide use in the world has caused an estimated 200 000 to 300 000 human poisonings annually and of these about 5 % are fatal. Examples of this problem are to be found in the literature (EPA, 1974; ICAITI, 1977; Pimentel *et al.*, 1978).

In addition, pesticides destroy beneficial species along with many pest species (Pimentel and Goodman, 1974; Brown, 1978a). Thus, natural enemies of pests are often eliminated during routine pesticide applications, and outbreaks of other pests occur because their natural biological control has been exterminated (van den Bosch and Messenger, 1973). When this happens, additional pesticide usually is applied to control the new pest. Not infrequently, and certainly following continuous application of powerful insecticides, the treated pest population evolves resistance to the pesticide. In fact, today about 367 species of pests and mites are considered resistant to pesticides (G. P. Georghiou (1976) personal communication).

At times pesticide applications not only kill pest and beneficial species, but their potent residues invade soil and waterways. In areas of the world where insecticides have been heavily applied to control agricultural pests, the malaria vector, *Anopheles* mosquitoes, that lived in the contaminated water, have evolved high levels of resistance to the insecticides. To control the mosquitoes, the level of insecticide used had to be increased two- to three-fold during the past four to five years (ICAITI, 1977). In this way the cycle of pesticide application, destruction of beneficial species, increased environmental pollution, increased resistance in pests and finally increased pesticide application has been a 'treadmill' – with no end in sight. The ultimate affect on crop production and food supplies will be greater inputs of energy for pest control.

The Future?

One is tempted to ask who is responsible for the shortages in food supplies. Who is responsible for the growing shortages of our major sources of energy? Who is responsible for environmental pollution? Man can not escape the answer that he, himself, has allowed his numbers to increase up to and even beyond the capacity of his biological environment to provide adequate supplies of needed resources (Brown, 1978b).

The best calculation is that if there were only about 1000 million humans on earth, all could enjoy a relatively high quality life. With the present world population above 4000 million world food and energy resources even now are being stretched to cover needs. How then can we expect that the same pool of resources will be able to provide amply for the more than 6000 million humans expected by 2000 A.D.? Perhaps we should abandon hope for a high quality life? Or perhaps we can acknowledge the problem now and begin to try to solve it.

The answer is not simply to produce more of the same crops we already grow. Our analysis has shown that even now energy, land and other biological resource limitations make it impossible to provide the present world population of 4000 million a U.S. per capita daily diet of 73 g of animal protein. The evidence suggests the standard of living in the world will have to be reduced to accommodate the rapidly growing numbers of human beings in the world. A substantial shift will have to be made in the diet. Less meat will be consumed while more grain, potatoes, beans and turnips will be eaten. The peoples of the developed world will have to join the other two-thirds, that include those peoples in China and India, in eating a more vegetarian-type diet.

More people will have to be crowded into smaller living quarters. Emphasis will be given to utilizing energy for essential purposes and less for pleasure. The overall trend will be a declining standard of living as the world population continues its growth beyond the biological carrying capacity of the earth.

Although man's scientific expertise will help alleviate some of the world shortages, science can not solve the problems the world faces today. To be convinced of this examine what progress has been made in improving the quality of life of the people of the developing countries during the past decade.

One action that is needed is for man to control his numbers. However, this 'task may well be the most difficult mankind ever faced' (NAS, 1971). If birth-rates are to be reduced on this massive scale, parents must understand that it is in their own and their progenies' best interest to have fewer children. This can be done only if the direct costs of children to parents were to increase, and socially acceptable substitutes for large families are developed. Within each society and ecological system, these difficult structural changes in society must be encouraged in conjunction with policies that augment food supplies, and improve health, education and lifestyle. Ultimately, it is up to each individual to reduce population growth. Clearly, if man does not control his numbers, nature will.

Appendix A

Fertilizers

Table A1 Energy inputs for nitrogen fertilizers (Mcal kgN^{-1}) (Lockeretz, 1978).

Type	Production				Transportation	Storage and transfer	Total
	Natural Gas	Fuel Oil	Electricity	Total			
Anhydrous ammonia	11.6	0	0.1	11.7	0.2	0.1	12.0
Urea (prilled or granular)	12.7	0	0.9	13.6	0.4	0.3	14.3
Ammonium nitrate (prilled or granular)	13.4	0	0.5	13.9	0.5	0.3	14.7

Table A2 Energy inputs for phosphate and potash fertilizers ($10^3 \times kcal\,kg^{-1}$ of P or K) (Lockeretz, 1978).

Type	Production	Transportation of raw materials	Transportation and distribution of final product
Phosphate rock	0.4	–	0.9
Normal superphosphate (0–20–0)	0.6	0.2	1.5
Triple superphosphate (0–46–0)	2.2	0.2	0.6
Potash (K_2O)	1.1	0.2	0.5

Table A3 Energy inputs for liming materials ($kcal\,kg^{-1}$) (Terhune, 1978).

Type	Mining	Manufacturing	Transportation of raw materials	Transportation and distribution of final product
Crushed and ground limestone	15.45	0	0	300
Burned limestone	15.45	1893	200	300
Hydrated lime	15.45	1893	200	300

Appendix B

Fuels

Table B1 Energy supplies and efficiency (Cervinka, 1978).

Energy source	Unit	Kcal unit^{-1}	Production inputs (kcal)	Total kcal unit^{-1}
Gasoline	Litre	8179	1930	10 109
Diesel	Litre	9235	2179	11 414
Fuel oil	Litre	9235	2179	11 414
Liquid petroleum gas	Litre	6234	1471	7705
Natural gas	m^3	9885	1928	11 813
Coal, hard	kg	7222	563	7785
Coal, soft	kg	7260	566	7826
Hardwood	kg	4600	345	4945
Softwood	kg	4200	315	4515
Electricity	kWh	859	2004	2863

Appendix C

Pesticides

The following section is taken from a report prepared by Pimentel (1978).

Table C1 Energy inputs for the basic production of various pesticides. All given as 1 kg active ingredient.

Pesticides	kcal for production	Source
Herbicides		
MCPA	30 952	Green (1976)
Diuron	64 290	Green "
Atrazine	45 240	Green "
Trifluralin	35 170	Green "
Paraquat	109 520	Green "
2,4-D	24 200	Pimentel (1973)
2,4,5-T	56 700	Green (1976)
Chloramben	71 400	Green "
Dinoseb	19 080	Green "
Propanil	52 240	Green "
Propachlor	69 050	Green "
Dicamba	70 240	Green "
Glyphosate	108 100	Green "
Diquat	95 240	Green "
Insecticides		
DDT	24 200	Leach and Slesser (1973)
Toxaphene	38 100	Green (1976)
Methyl Parathion	13 810	Green "
Carbofuran	108 100	Green "
Carbaryl	36 430	Green "
Fumigants		
Methyl bromide	15 950	Steinhart and Steinhart (1974b)
Fungicides		
Ferbam	15 250	Green (1976)
Maneb	23 570	Green "
Captan	27 380	Green "
Sulfur	26 620	Fritsch et al. (1975)
Pesticide Average	49 020*	

* The percentage of oil, natural gas and coal involved in the production of pesticides has been calculated as 42 % oil, 38 % natural gas and 20 % coal.

Table C2 Energy inputs (production, formulation, packaging, transport) for various pesticides. All values given for 1 kg active pesticide ingredient.

Pesticide	Production active ingredient[a]	Formulation	Packaging	Transport[h]	Total	% of energy types Oil	Gas	Coal
Herbicide								
Miscible oil	57 000	33 300[b]	8500[e]	1110	99 910	60	23	17
Wettable powder	57 000	2500[c]	2600[f]	670	62 770	43	37	20
Granules	57 000	3600[d]	20 000[g]	6720	86 600	42	37	21
Insecticide								
Miscible oil	44 000	33 300[b]	8500[e]	1110	86 910	61	23	16
Wettable powder	44 000	2500[c]	2600[f]	670	61 470	43	37	20
Granules	44 000	3600[d]	20 000[g]	6720	85 300	42	37	21
Dust	44 000	3600[d]	20 000[g]	6720	85 300	42	37	21
Fungicide								
Miscible oil	22 000	33 300[b]	8500[e]	1110	64 910	70	15	15
Wettable powder	22 000	2500[c]	2600[f]	670	27 770	42	37	21
Granules	22 000	3600[d]	20 000[g]	6720	51 600	41	37	22
Dust	22 000	3600[d]	20 000[g]	6720	51 600	41	37	22

(a) Average from Table C1. (b) Assumes a 30 % formulation. (c) Assumes a 50 % wettable powder. (d) Assumes 5 % active ingredient in either granules or dust. (e) Packaging includes a metal 5 gal container and is based on data of Berry and Makino (1974). (f) Assumes pesticide formulation in 1 kg paper packages and is based on data from Berry and Makino (1974). (g) Assumes pesticide formulation in 20 kg paper packages and is based on data from Berry and Makino (1974). (h) Assumed 0.53 kcal kg^{-1} km^{-1} for transport by truck and rail and at a mean distance of 640 km.

Further Reading

Chapter 1

COTTRELL, F. (1955). *Energy and Society*. Greenwood Press, Westport, Connecticut. 330 pp.

LEACH, G. (1976). *Energy and Food Production*. IPC Science and Technology Press Limited, Guilford, Surrey. 137 pp.

WHITE, L. A. (1943). Energy and the evolution of culture. *Am. Anthropol.*, **45**, 335–354.

Chapter 2

COOK, E. (1976). *Man, Energy, Society*. W. H. Freeman, San Francisco. 478 pp.

HUBBERT, M. K. (1972). *Man's conquest of energy: its ecological and human consequences*. The environmental and ecological forum 1970–1971. pp. 1–50. U.S. Atomic Energy Commission, Office of Information Services. Oak Ridge, Tenn.

STEINHART, C. and STEINHART, J. (1974). *Energy Sources, Use and Role in Human Affairs*. Duxbury Press, North Scituate, Mass. 362 pp.

Chapter 3

SCHNEIDER, S. H. (1976). *The Genesis Strategy: Climate and Global Survival*. Plenum, New York. 419 pp.

SOUTHWOOD, T. R. E. (1966). *Ecological Methods*. Methuen, London. 391 pp.

Chapter 4

CLARK, C. and HASWELL, M. (1970). The Economics of Subsistence Agriculture. MacMillan, London. 267 pp.

LEE, R. B. (1969). !Kung bushman subsistence: an input-output analysis. pp. 47–79. In *Environment and Cultural Behavior: Ecological Studies in Cultural Anthropology*. A. P. Vayda (ed.). Natural History Press, Garden City, New York.

RAPPAPORT, R. A. (1968). *Pigs for the Ancestors: Ritual in the Ecology of a New Guinea People*. Yale University Press. 311 pp.

Chapter 5

DESHLER, W. W. (1965). Native cattle keeping in Eastern Africa. pp. 153–68. In *Man, Culture and Animals*. A. Leeds and A. P. Vayda, eds. AAAS Publ. # 78, Washington, D. C.

LEONARD, J. N. (1973). *The First Farmers*. The Emergence of Man Series, Time-Life Books, New York. 160 pp.

RAPPAPORT, R. A. (1968). *Pigs for the Ancestors: Ritual in the Ecology of a New Guinea People*. Yale University Press. 311 pp.

Chapter 6

PIMENTEL, D., DRITSCHILO, W., KRUMMEL, J. and KUTZMAN, J. (1975). Energy and land constraints in food-protein production. *Science*, **190**, 754–61.

REID, J. T. (1970). Will meat, milk and egg production be possible in the future? pp. 50–63. In *Proc. Cornell Nutrition Conference for Feed Manufacturers*. Buffalo, N. Y., November.

Chapter 7

LEACH, G. (1976). *Energy and Food Production*. IPC Science and Technology Press Limited, Guilford, Surrey. 137 pp.

PIMENTEL, D. (1976). Crisi energetica e agricoltura. pp. 251–66. In *Enciclopeida della Scienza e della Tecnica*. Mondadori, Milan.

PIMENTEL, D., HURD, L. E., BELLOTTI, A. C., FORSTER, M. J., OKA, I. N., SHOLES, O. D. and WHITMAN, R. J. (1973). Food production and the energy crisis. *Science*, **182**, 443–49.

Chapter 8

LEACH, G. (1976). Energy and Food Production. IPC Science and Technology Press Limited, Guilford, Surrey. 137 pp.

PIMENTEL, D. (1976). Crisi energetica e agricoltura. pp. 251–66. In *Enciclopedia della Scienza e della Tecnica*. Mondadori, Milan.

Chapter 9

RAWITSCHER, M. and MAYER, J. (1977). Nutritional outputs and energy inputs in seafoods. *Science*, **198**, 261–64.

ROCHEREAU, S. and PIMENTEL, D. (1978). Energy trade-offs between Northeast fishery production and coastal power reactors. *Energy*, **3**, 575–589.

Chapter 10

BERRY, R. S. and MAKINO, H. (1974). Energy thrift in packaging and marketing. *Tech. Rev.,* **76** (**4**), 32–43.
REVELLE, R. (1976). Energy use in rural India. *Science,* **192**, 969–75.

Chapter 11

HIRST, E. (1972). *Energy consumption for transportation in the U.S.* Oak Ridge National Laboratory, Oak Ridge, Tennessee. 38 pp.

Chapter 12

BROWN, L. R. (1978). *The Twenty Ninth Day.* W. W. Norton, New York. 363 pp.
KEYFITZ, N. (1976). World resources and the world middle class. *Sci. Am.,* **235**(**1**), 28–35.
PIMENTEL, D. (ed.). (1977). *World Food, Pest Losses, and the Environment.* Westview Press, Boulder, Colorado. 206 pp.
SCHNEIDER, S. H. (1976). *The Genesis Strategy: Climate and Global Survival.* Plenum, New York. 419 pp.

Appendices

STEINHART, J. S. and STEINHART, C. E. (1974). Energy use in the U.S. food system. *Science,* **184**, 306–316.

References

AED (1960). Cost of production of corn. Agricultural Economics Division, Department of Agriculture and National Resources, Manila, *Agr. Ser.*, # **2**. 24 pp.

AKINWUMI, J. A. (1971). Costs and returns in commercial maize production in the derived savanna belt of Western State, Nigeria. *Bull. Rural Econ. and Social., Ibadan*, **6**(2), 219–51.

ALLAN, P. (1961). Fertilisers and food in Asia and the Far East. *Span*, **4**, 32–35.

ALTSCHUL, A. M. (ed.) (1958). *Processed Plant Protein Foodstuffs.* Academic Press, New York. 955 pp.

AUDY, J. R. (ed.). (1964). *Public Health and Medical Sciences in the Pacific – a Forty-year Review.* Pacific Science Congress, 10th, Honolulu, Univ. of Hawaii Press. 134 pp.

BATTY, J. C. and KELLER, J. (1979). Energy requirements for irrigation in *Energy in Agriculture*. D. Pimentel (ed.). CRC Handbook Series, CRC Press, West Palm Beach, Florida. In press.

BDPA. (1965). *Techniques Rurales en Afrique.* Les temps de travaux. Bureau pour le Développement de la Production Agricole (BDPA). Republique Francaise, Ministere de la Cooperation. 384 pp.

BEASLEY, R. P. (1972). *Erosion and Sediment Pollution Control.* Iowa State University Press, Ames. 320 pp.

BELL, F. W. and HAZLETON, J. E. (eds). (1967). *Recent Developments and Research in Fisheries Economics.* Oceana Publications, New York.

BENNETT, H. H. (1939). *Soil Conservation.* McGraw-Hill, New York. 993 pp.

BERRY, R. S. and FELS, M. F. (1973). *The Production and Consumption of Automobiles.* An energy analysis of the manufacture, discard, and reuse of the automobile and its component materials. Department of Chemistry, Univ. of Chicago, Chicago, Ill. 56 pp.

BERRY, R. S. and MAKINO, H. (1974). Energy thrift in packaging and marketing. *Tech. Rev.*, **76**(4), 1–13; 32–43.

BEWS, J. W. (1973). *Human Ecology.* Russell and Russell, New York. 312 pp.

BLAXTER, K. (1978). What happens to farming when the fossil fuels run out? *Farmer's Weekly*, Jan. 20.

BRODRICK, A. H. (1949). *Lascaux. A Commentary.* Lindsay Drummond Ltd., London.

BROWN, A. W. A. (1978a). *Ecology of Pesticides*. John Wiley and Sons, New York. 525 pp.

BROWN, L. R. (1978b). *The Twenty Ninth Day*. W. W. Norton, New York. 363 pp.

BROWN, L. R. (1978c). The global economic prospect: new sources of economic stress. *Worldwatch Paper*, **20**, Worldwatch Institute, Washington, D.C. 56 pp.

BROWN, L. R. and ECKHOLM, E. P. (1974). *By Bread Alone*. Praeger, New York. 272 pp.

BROWN, L. R., McGRATH, P. L. and STOKES, B. (1976). Twenty-two dimensions of the population problem. *Worldwatch Paper*, **5**, Worldwatch Institute. 83 pp.

BRYSON, R. A. (1974). A perspective on climatic change. *Science*, **184**, 753–60.

BRYSON, R. A. and WENDLAND, W. M. (1975). Climatic effects of atmospheric pollution. pp. 139–47 in *The Changing Global Environment*. S. F. Singer, (ed.). D. Reidel, Dordrecht, Holland.

BURGES, A. and RAW, F. (eds). (1967). *Soil Biology*. Academic Press, New York. 532 pp.

BURINGH, P., VAN HEEMST, H. D. J. and STARING, G. J. (1975). Computation of the absolute maximum food production of the world. *Agr. Univ., Dept. Trop. Soil Sci.* (Wageningen).

BURTON, B. T. (1965). *The Heinz Handbook of Nutrition*. McGraw-Hill, New York. 462 pp.

BYERLY, T. C. (1966). The relation of animal agriculture to world food shortages. pp. 31–63 in *Proc. 15th Ann. Mtg. Agr. Res. Inst.*, October, 1966. National Academy of Sciences, Washington, D.C.

CAPTIVA, F. J. (1968). Modern U.S. shrimp vessels design, construction, current trends and future developments. pp. 141–44 in *The Future of the Fishing Industry of the United States*, G. DeWitt (ed.), Univ. Washington, Publ. in Fisheries – New Series. Vol. **4**. 346 pp.

CASPER, M. E. (ed.). (1977). *Energy Saving Techniques for the Food Industry*. Noyes Data Corp., Park Ridge, N.J. 657 pp.

CERVINKA, V., CHANCELLOR, W. J., COFFELT, R. J., CURLEY, R. G. and DOBIE, J. B. (1974). *Energy Requirements for Agriculture in California*. Calif. Dept. Food and Agr., Univ. Calif., Davis. 151 pp.

CERVINKA, V. (1979). Energy supplies and efficiency. In *Energy in Agriculture*. D. Pimentel, (ed.). CRC Handbook Series, CRC Press, West Palm Beach, Florida. In press.

CLARK, C. and HASWELL, M. (1970). *The Economics of Subsistence Agriculture*. MacMillan, London. 267 pp.

CONNELL, K. H. (1950). *The Population of Ireland, 1750–1845*. Clarendon Press, Oxford. 293 pp.

References   153

444

COOK, E. (1976). *Man, Energy, Society*. W. H. Freeman, San Francisco. 478 pp.

CORSA, L. and OAKLEY, D. (1971). Consequences of population growth for health services in less developed countries – an initial appraisal. pp. 368–402 in *Rapid Population Growth*. Vol. II. Research Papers. National Academy of Sciences. Johns Hopkins Press, Baltimore. 690 pp.

COTTRELL, F. (1955). *Energy and Society*. Greenwood Press, Westport, Connecticut. 330 pp.

CRAMER, H. H. (1967). Plant protection and world crop production. *Pflanzenschutznachrichten*, **20**(1), 1–524.

DeFEVER, A. (1968). Modern U.S. tuna vessel construction, design and future trends. pp. 134–40 in *The Future of the Fishing Industry of the United States*, G. DeWitt (ed.), Univ. Washington, Publ. in Fisheries – New Series. Vol. **4**. 346 pp.

DE LOS REYES, B. N., QUINTANA, E. V., TORRES, R. D., ELA, O. M., FORTUNA, N. M. and MARASIGAN, J. M. (1965). A case study of the tractor- and carabao-cultivated lowland rice farms in Laguna, crop year 1962–63. *Phil. Agr.*, **49**(2), 75–94.

DESHLER, W. W. (1965). Native cattle keeping in Eastern Africa. pp. 153–68 in *Man, Culture and Animals*. A. Leeds and A. P. Vayda, (eds). AAAS Publ. #78, Washington, D.C.

DIETRICH, R. F. (1975). Shopping smart. *Progressive Grocer*, **54**(4), 48–50, 52.

DOERING, O. (1977). The energy balance of food legume production. pp. 725–732 in *Energy Use Management*. R. A. Fazzolare and C. B. Smith, (eds). Vol. I. Pergamon, New York.

ECKHOLM, E. P. (1976). *Losing Ground. Environmental Stress and World Food Prospects*. Norton, New York. 223 pp.

EDWARDSON, W. (1975). *Energy Analysis and the Fishing Industry*. A report of the Energy Analysis Unit, University of Strathclyde, Glasgow.

ELTON, C. S. (1927). *Animal Ecology*. Sidgwick and Jackson, Ltd., London, 207 pp.

EOP (1977). *The National Energy Plan*. Executive Office of the President, Energy Policy and Planning. U. S. Government Printing Office, Washington, D. C. 103 pp.

EPA (1974) *Strategy of the Environmental Protection Agency for Controlling the Adverse Effects of Pesticides*. Environmental Protection Agency, Office of Pesticide Programs, Office of Water and Hazardous Materials, Washington, D. C. 36 pp.

ERNST, E. (1978). Fuel consumption among rural families in Upper Volta, West Africa. *Eighth World Forestry Congress*. (In press).

FAKHRY, A. (1969). *The Pyramids*. University of Chicago Press, Chicago, 272 pp.

154   References

FAO (1961). *Production Yearbook 1960*. Vol. 14. Food and Agriculture Organization, U.N., Rome. 507 pp.

FAO (1963) *Basic study #11. Third World food survey*. FAO, U.N., Rome. 102 pp.

FAO (1966) *Rice: Grain of Life. World Food Problems No. 6*. FAO, U.N., Rome. 93 pp.

FAO (1972a). *FAO Catalogue of Fishing Gear Designs*. Fishing News (Books) Ltd., London.

FAO (1972b). *Atlas of the Living Resources of the Seas*. FAO Dept. of Fisheries, FAO of U.N., Rome.

FAO (1973). *Yearbook of Fishery Statistics 1972. Vol. 35*. FAO, U.N., Rome. 328 pp.

FAO (1976). *Yearbook of Fishery Statistics 1975. Vol. 40*. Food and Agriculture Organization of the United Nations. 334 pp.

FAO (1977) *Production Yearbook 1976. Vol. 30*. FAO, U.N. Rome.

FDA (1974). *Current Levels for Natural or Unavoidable Defects in Food for Human Use That Present No Health Hazard*. Food and Drug Administration, Dept. of HEW, PHS, Rockville Md. (Fifth revision). 10 pp.

FEA (1975). *Energy Consumption in the Food System*. Federal Energy Administration, Rept. No. 13392-007-001, prepared for FEA Industrial Technology Office by Booz, Allen and Hamilton, Inc., Bethesda, Dec. 1.

FEA (1976a). *Energy and U.S. agriculture: 1974 data base. Vol. 1*. Federal Energy Administration. U.S. Government Printing Office, Washington, D.C.

FEA (1976b) *National Energy Outlook*. Federal Energy Administration, FEA-N-75/713. U.S. Government Printing Office, Washington, D.C. 323 pp.

FORBES, R. J. (1968). *The Conquest of Nature*. Frederick Praeger, New York. 98 pp.

FRANKEL, O. H. (1971). Genetic dangers in the green revolution. *Wld. Agr.*, **19**, 9–13.

FREEMAN, J. D. (1955). *Iban Agriculture*. Her Majesty's Stationery Office, London. 148 pp.

FRITSCH, *et al.* (1975). *Energy Impact Control Policies*. Energy Impact Report, Department of Food and Agriculture, California. Draft Report, October 28, 1977.

GERTEL, K. and WOLLMAN, N. (1960). Rural-urban competition for water: price and assessment guides to western water allocation. *J. Farm Econ.*, **42(5)**, 1332–44.

GRANT, W. R. and MULLINS, T. (1963). Enterprise costs and returns on rice farms in Grant Prairie, Ark. *Ark. Ag. Exp. Sta. Rep. Series*, **119**. 35 pp.

GRANT, W. R., AMAREL, R. E. and JOHNSON, S. S. (1971). Leasing on California rice farms. *Info. Ser. Agr. Econ.*, **71–2.** Univ. Calif., Davis.

GREEN, M. B. (1976). *Energy in Agriculture.* Chem. and Industry. August 641–46.

GULLAND, J. A. (1971). *The Fish Resources of the Ocean.* Fishing News (Books) Ltd., London (for FAO of U.N.).

GULLAND, J. A. (1974). *The Management of Marine Fisheries.* University of Washington Press, Seattle.

HAMMOND, A. L. (1972). Energy options: challenge for the future. *Science*, **177,** 875–876.

HANDLER, P. (ed.). (1970). *Biology and the Future of Man.* Oxford Univ. Press, Oxford.

HARGROVE, T. R. (1972). *Agricultural Research: Impact on Environment.* Spec. Rep. 69, Agr. & Home Econ. Exp. Sta., Iowa State Univ. of Science and Technology, Ames, Iowa.

HARPER, J. L. (1977). *Population Biology of Plants.* Academic Press, London. 892 pp.

HARRAR, J. G. (1961). Socio-economic factors that limit needed food production and consumption. *Fed. Proc.*, **20,** 381–83.

HCP. (1974). *Handbook of Chemistry and Physics.* The Chemical Rubber Co., Cleveland, Ohio.

HEICHEL, G. (1979). Energy attributable to seed. In *Energy in Agriculture.* D. Pimentel (ed.). CRC Handbook Series, CRC Press, West Palm Beach, Florida. In press.

HENRY, K. A. (1971). *Atlantic Menhaden (Brevoortia tyrannus) Resource and Fishery – Analysis of Decline.* Technical Report, National Marine Fisheries Service, Seattle, Washington. August. 39 pp.

HERTZBERG, R., VAUGHAN, B. and GREENE, J. (1973). *Putting Food By.* Stephen Greene Press, Brattleboro, Vt. 360 pp.

HIRST, E. (1972). *Energy Consumption for Transportation in the U.S.* Oak Ridge National Laboratory, Oak Ridge, Tennessee. 38 pp.

HIRST, E. (1974). Food-related energy requirements. *Science*, **184,** 134–39.

HUBBERT, M. K. (1972). Man's conquest of energy: its ecological and human consequences. *The environmental and ecological forum 1970–1971.* pp. 1–50. U.S. Atomic Energy Commission, Office of Information Services. Oak Ridge, Tenn.

ICAITI (1977). *An Environmental and Economic Study of the Consequences of Pesticide Use in Central American Cotton Production.* Central America Research Institute for Industry. United Nations Environment Programme. Final Report. 273 pp.

INGRAHAM, E. W. (1975). *A Query into the Quarter Century.* On the interrelationships of food, people, environment, land and climate. Wright-Ingraham Institute, Colorado Springs, Colo. 47 pp.

INSTITUTE OF ECOLOGY. (1972). *Man in the Living Environment.* The Univ. of Wisconsin Press, Madison, Wisconsin. 288 pp.

JENSEN, L. B. (1949). *Meat and Meat Foods*. Ronald Press, N.Y. 218 pp.

JILER, H. (1972). *Commodity Yearbook*. Commodity Research Bureau, New York.

KEARL, C. D. (1962). *Field Crops Costs and Returns from Farm Cost Accounts*. N.Y. Cornell Agr. Exp. Sta., Dept. Agr. Econ. A. E. Research **102**. November. 21 pp.

KELLOGG, W. W. (1975). Climate change and the influence of man's activities on the global environment. pp. 13–23. In *The Changing Global Environment*. S. F. Singer, (ed.). D. Reidel, Dordrecht, Holland.

KEVAN, D. K. McE. (1962). *Soil Animals*. Philosophical Library, New York. 237 pp.

KEYFITZ, N. (1976). World resources and the world middle class. *Sci. Am.*, **235**[1], 28–35.

KOVDA, V. A. (1971). The problem of biological and economic productivity of the earth's land areas. *Soviet Geogr.: Rev. and Trans.*, **12**[1], 6–23.

LAYCOCK, G. (1966). *The Alien Animals*. The Natural History Press, Garden City, N.Y. 240 pp.

LEACH. G. (1976). *Energy and Food Production*. IPC Science and Technology Press Limited, Guilford, Surrey. 137 pp.

LEACH, G. and M. SLESSER. (1973). *Energy Equivalents of Network Input to Food Producing Processes*. Strathclyde University, Glasgow. 38 pp.

LEE, N. E. (1955). *Travel and Transport Through the Ages*. Cambridge University Press, Cambridge, England. 187 pp.

LEE, R. B. (1969). !Kung bushman subsistence: an input-output analysis. pp. 47–79. In *Environment and Cultural Behavior: Ecological Studies in Cultural Anthropology*. A. P. Vayda (ed.). Natural History Press, Garden City, New York.

LEE, R. B. and DeVORE, I. (eds.). (1976). *Kalahari Hunter-Gatherers*. Harvard University Press, Cambridge, Mass. 408 pp.

LEONARD, J. N. (1973). *The First Farmers*. The Emergence of Man Series, Time-Life Books, New York. 160 pp.

LEWIS, O. (1951). *Life in a Mexican village: Tepoztlán restudied*. University of Illinois Press, Urbana, 512 pp.

LOCKERETZ, W. (1979). Energy inputs for nitrogen, phosphorus, and potash fertilizers. In *Energy in Agriculture*. D. Pimentel (ed.). CRC Handbook Series, CRC Press, West Palm Beach, Florida. In press.

MACK, J. (1971). *Catfish Farming Handbook*. Educator Books, San Angelo, Texas. 195 pp.

MALLORY, W. H. (1928). *China: Land of Famine*. American Geographical Society, New York. 199 pp.

MALONE, T. (1974). *Transcript of National Academy of Sciences Luncheon Meeting*, May 28.

MANGELSDORF, P. C. (1966). Genetic potentials for increasing yields of food crops and animals. In *Prospects of the World Food Supply.* Symp. Proc. Natl. Acad. Sci., Washington, D. C.

MARGETTS, A. R. (1974). Modern development of fishing gear. pp. 243–60 In *Sea Fisheries Research.* F. R. Harden Jones (ed.). John Wiley and Sons, New York.

MARSHALL, L. J. (1976). *The !Kung of Nyae Nyae.* Harvard University Press, Cambridge, Mass. 408 pp.

MATSUBAYASHI, M., ITO, R., NAMOTO, T., TAKASE T. and YAMADA, N. (1963) *Theory and Practice of Growing Rice.* Tokyo, Fuji Publ. Co. 520 pp.

MFACDCGI. (1966). *Farm Management in India.* Directorate of Econ. and Stat., Dept. of Agr., Ministry of Food, Agriculture Community Development and Cooperation Government of India (MFACDCGI). 128 pp.

MORISON, T. (1911). *The Industrial Organization of an Indian Province.* John Murray, London. 347 pp.

MULLINS, T. and GRANT, W. R. (1968). Enterprise costs and returns on rice farms in the Delta, Ark. *Rep. Ser. Ark. Agr. Exp. Sta.*, # 170. 26 pp.

NAS (1971). *Rapid Population Growth. Vols.* I, II. Published for NAS by Johns Hopkins Press, Baltimore, MD. 105 and 690 pp.

NAS (1974a). *Productive Agriculture and a Quality Environment.* National Academy of Sciences, Washington, D.C. 189 pp.

NAS (1974b). *Vegetarian Diets.* A Statement of the Food and Nutrition Board, National Research Council. Committee on Nutritional Misinformation. National Academy of Sciences, Washington, D.C.

NAS (1975). *Population and Food: Crucial Issues.* National Academy of Sciences, Washington, D.C. 50 pp.

NAS (1977). *Supporting Papers: World Food and Nutrition Study. Vol.* II. National Academy of Sciences, Washington, D.C. 297 pp.

NEF, J. V. (1977). An early energy crisis and its consequences. *Sci. Am.*, **237[5]**, 140–51.

OECD (1974). *Meat Balances in OECD Member Countries 1959–1972.* Organization for Economic Cooperation and Development, Paris.

PATHAK, M. D. (1975). Utilization of insect-plant interactions in pest control. pp. 121–48. In *Insects, Science and Society.* D. Pimentel, (ed.). Academic Press, New York. 284 pp.

PENNER, S. S. and ICERMAN, L. (1974) *Energy. Vol.* I. *Demands, resources, impact, technology, and policy.* Addison-Wesley, Reading, Mass.

158   *References*

PEP(1955). *World Population and Resources.* Political and Economic Planning, London. 339 pp.

PIMENTEL, D. (1961). Animal population regulation by the genetic feedback mechanism. *Am. Nat.,* **95**, 65–79.

PIMENTEL, D. (1968). Population regulation and genetic feedback. *Science,* **159**, 1432–1437.

PIMENTEL, D.(1973). Data obtained from an engineer at a pesticide manufacturing plant who wanted to remain anonymous.

PIMENTEL, D. (1974). Energy use in world food production. *Environ. Biol. Report,* **74**–1, Cornell University, Ithaca, N.Y. 43 pp.

PIMENTEL, D. (1976). Crisi energetica e agricoltura. pp. 251–66. In *Enciclopedia della Scienza e della Tecnica.* Mondadori, Milan.

PIMENTEL, D. (ed.). (1977). *World Food, Pest Losses, and the Environment.* Westview Press, Boulder, Colorado. 206 pp.

PIMENTEL, D. (1979). Energy inputs for the production, formulation, packaging and transport of various pesticides. In *Energy in Agriculture.* D. Pimentel, (ed.). CRC Handbook Series, CRC Press, West Palm Beach, Florida. In press.

PIMENTEL, D., ANDOW, D., DYSON-HUDSON, R., GALLAHAN, D., JACOBSEN, S., IRISH, M., KROOP, S., MOSS, A., SCHREINER, I., SHEPARD, M., THOMPSON, T. and VINZANT, W.(1979). *Environmental and Social Costs of Pesticide use.* Manuscript.

PIMENTEL, D. and BEYER, N. (1976). *Energy Inputs in Indian Agriculture.* Unpublished data.

PIMENTEL, D., and DRITSCHILO, W., KRUMMEL J. and KUTZMAN, J. (1975). Energy and land constraints in food-protein production. *Science,* **190**, 754–61.

PIMENTEL, D. and GOODMAN, N. (1974). Environmental impact of pesticides. pp. 25–52. In *Survival in Toxic Environments.* M. A. Q. Khan and J. P. Bederka (eds). Academic Press, New York. 553 pp.

PIMENTEL, D., HURD, L. E., BELLOTTI, A. C., FORSTER, M. J., OKA, I. N., SHOLES, O. D. and WHITMAN, R. J.(1973). Food production and the energy crisis. *Science,* **182**, 443–49.

PIMENTEL, D., LYNN, W. R., MacREYNOLDS, W. K., HEWES, M. T. and RUSH, S. (1974). *Workshop on Research Methodologies for Studies of Energy, Food, Man and Environment. Phase I.* Center for Environmental Quality Management. Cornell University, Ithaca, New York. 52 pp.

PIMENTEL, D., NAFUS, D., VERGARA, W., PAPAJ, D., JACONETTA, L., WULFE, M., OLSVIG, L., FRECH, K., LOYE, M. and MENDOZA, E. (1978). Biological solar energy conversion and U.S. energy policy. *Bioscience,* **28**, 376–382.

PIMENTEL, D., OLTENACU, P. A., KRUMMEL, J., ALLEN, M. and NESHEIM, M. (1978a). Unpublished data.

PIMENTEL, D., OLTENACU, P. A., NESHEIM, M., KRUMMEL, J. and ALLEN, M. S. (1978b). *Livestock Production Systems: Energy and Land Conservation.* Manuscript.

PIMENTEL, D., TERHUNE, E. C., DYSON-HUDSON, R., ROCHEREAU, S., SAMIS, R., SMITH, E., DENMAN, D., REIFSCHNEIDER, D. and SHEPARD, M. (1976). Land degradation: effects on food and energy resources. *Science*, **194**, 149–55.

PIMENTEL, D., TERHUNE, E. C., DRITSCHILO, W., GALLAHAN, D., KINNER, N., NAFUS, D., PETERSON, R., ZAREH, N., MISITI, J. and HABER-SCHAIM, O. (1977). Pesticides, insects in foods, and cosmetic standards, *Bioscience*, **27**, 178–85.

PRADHAN, S. (1971). Revolution in pest control. *World Sci. News*, **8**, 41–7.

PSAC (1967). *The World Food Problem. Vols.* **I, II, III**. Report of Panel on the World Food Supply, President's Science Advisory Committee, the White House. U.S. Government Printing Office, Washington, D.C.

PYKE, M. (1970). *Man and Food.* McGraw Hill, New York. 256 pp.

RAPPAPORT, R. A. (1968). *Pigs for the Ancestors: Ritual in the Ecology of a New Guinea People.* Yale University Press. 311 pp.

RAPPAPORT, R. A. (1971). The flow of energy in an agricultural society. *Sci. Am.*, **225**(3), 116–32.

RAWITSCHER, M. and MAYER, J. (1977). Nutritional outputs and energy inputs in seafoods. *Science*, **198**, 261–64.

REGISTER, W. D. and SONNEBURG, L. M. (1973). The vegetarian diet. *J. Am. Diet. Assn.*, **62**, 253.

REID, J. T. (1970). Will meat, milk and egg production be possible in the future? pp. 50–63. In *Proc. Cornell Nutrition Conference for Feed Manufacturers*, Buffalo, N.Y., November.

REIFSNYDER, W. E. and LULL, H. W. (1965). Radiant energy in relation to forests. *Tech. Bull. No.* **1344**. U.S. Dept. Agr., Forest Service. 111 pp.

REVELLE, R. (1976). Energy use in rural India. *Science*, **192**, 969–75.

ROBERTS, L. W. (1976). Improving the production and nutritional quality of food legumes. pp. 309–317. In *Nutrition and Agricultural Development*. N. S. Scrimshaw and M. Béhar (eds). Plenum, New York.

ROCHEREAU, S. P. (1976). *Energy analysis and coastal shelf resource management: nuclear power generation vs. seafood protein production in the Northeast region of the U.S.* Ph.D. thesis, Cornell University, 190 pp.

ROCHEREAU, S. and PIMENTEL, D. (1978). Energy tradeoffs between Northeast fishery production and coastal power reactors. *J. Energy*, **3**, 545–89.

RSAS (1975). *Energy Uses.* Presented at Energy Conference, Aspenäs-

160   References

gården, Oct. 27–31, Royal Swedish Academy of Sciences. 80 pp.

RUSSELL, B. (1961). *An Outline of Philosophy*. World Publishing, Cleveland.

RUTHENBERG, H. (ed.). (1968). *Smallholder Farming Development in Tanzania*. Weltforum Verlag Munchen, Germany. 360 pp.

RUTHENBERG, H. (1971). *Farming Systems in the Tropics*. Clarendon Press, Oxford. 313 pp.

SAHLINS, M. (1972). *Stone Age Economics*. Aldine-Atherton, Chicago. 348 pp.

SCHNEIDER, S. H. (1976). *The Genesis Strategy: Climate and Global Survival*. Plenum, New York. 419 pp.

SERVICE, E. R. (1962). *Primitive Social Organization*. Random House, New York. 211 pp.

SINGER, S. F. (1975). Environmental effects of energy production. pp. 25–44. In *The Changing Global Environment*. S. F. Singer (ed.). D. Reidel, Dordrecht, Holland.

SMERDON, E. T. (1974). *Energy Conservation Practices in Irrigated Agriculture*. Sprinkler Irrigation Assn. Ann. Tech. Conf., Denver, Colorado.

SNYDER, D. P. (1976). Field crops costs and returns from farm cost accounts. *Agr. Econ. Res.*, **76-25**. Cornell Univ. Agr. Exp. Sta., Ithaca.

SNYDER, D. P. (1977). Cost of production – update for 1976 – on muck onions, potatoes, sweet corn, dry beans, apples. *Agr. Econ. Res.*, **77-11**. Cornell Univ. Agr. Exp. Sta., Ithaca.

SOEC (1976). *Eurostat – Energy Statistics Yearbook 1970–1975*. Statistical Office of the European Communities. Federal Republic of West Germany.

SOUTHWOOD, T. R. E. (1978). *Ecological Methods*. 2nd edition. Chapman and Hall, London. 530 pp.

SPENGLER, J. J. (1968). World hunger: past, present, prospective 'That there should be great famine.' *World Rev. Nutr. Diet.*, **9**, 1–31.

SRI (1972). *Patterns of Energy Consumption in the United States*. Stanford Research Institute, U.S. Government Printing Office, Washington, D.C.

STADELMAN, R. (1940). Maize cultivation in northwestern Guatemala. Compiled by the Carnegie Institution of Washington. *Contributions to American Anthropology and History, No.* **33**. *Carnegie Institute of Washington Pub.*, **523**, 83–263.

STANFORD, G. (1977). *Energy Conservation*. Agro-City Inc., Cedar Hill, Texas. Mimeo. 1 p.

STEINHART, C. and STEINHART, J. (1974a). *Energy Sources, Use and Role in Human Affairs*. Duxbury Press, North Scituate, Mass. 362 pp.

STEINHART, J. S. and STEINHART, C. E. (1974b). Energy use in the U.S. food system. *Science*, **184**, 306–16.

TANDON, B. N., RAMACHANDRAN, K., SHARMA, M. P. and VINAYAK, V. K. (1972). Nutritional survey in rural population of Kumaon Hill area, North India. *Am. J. Clin. Nutr.*, **25**(4), 432–436.

TERHUNE, E. (1977). Energy use in crop production: vegetables. pp. 769–78. In *Energy Use Management*. R. A. Fazzolare and C. B. Smith (eds). Vol. I. Pergamon, New York.

TERHUNE, E. (1979). Energy used in the U.S. for agricultural liming materials. In *Energy in Agriculture*. D. Pimentel (ed.). CRC Handbook Series, CRC Press, West Palm Beach, Florida. In press.

THURSTON, H. D. (1969). Tropical agriculture. A key to the world food crises. *BioScience*, **19**, 29–34.

UN (1957–71). *Statistical Yearbooks*. Statistical Office of the United Nations, Department of Economic and Social Affairs, New York.

UN (1973). World population prospects as assessed in 1968. *Population Studies, No.* **53**, Department of Economic and Social Affairs, United Nations.

UN (1974). Assessment of the World Food Situation. *United Nations World Food Conference*, November. FAO, Rome.

USBC (1975). *Statistical abstract of the United States 1975*. U.S. Bureau of the Census (U.S. Dept. of Commerce). 96th ed. U.S. Government Printing Office, Washington, D.C.

USBC (1976). *Statistical Abstract of the United States 1976*. U.S. Bureau of the Census (U.S. Dept. of Commerce). 97th ed. U.S. Government Printing Office, Washington, D.C.

USDA (1965). Losses in agriculture. *U.S. Department of Agriculture, Agr. Res. Serv. Handb. No.* **291**.

USDA (1971). *Agricultural Statistics, 1971*. U.S. Government Printing Office. 639 pp.

USDA (1971a). Agriculture and the environment. *Econ. Res. Serv., No.* **481**.

USDA (1971b). Fertilizer situation. *USDA, Econ. Res. Ser.*, FS–1. 42 pp.

USDA (1974a). Fertilizer situation. *Econ. Res. Ser., Rep. No.* FS–4. 24 pp.

USDA (1974b). Farmers' use of pesticides in 1971 . . . quantities. *Econ. Res. Serv., Agr. Econ. Rep., No.* **252**. 56 pp.

USDA (1974c). Our land and water resources, current and prospective supplies and uses. *Econ. Res. Serv. Misc. Publ., No.* **1290**.

USDA (1975a). *Agricultural Statistics 1975*. U.S. Government Printing Office, Washington, D.C.

USDA (1975b). National food situation. *Econ. Res. Serv.*, NFS–151.

USDA (1975c). Nutritive value of American foods in common units. *Agr. Res. Serv., Agr. Handbook, No.* **456**. 291 pp.

USDA (1976a). *Agricultural Statistics 1976*. U.S. Department of Agriculture, U.S. Government Printing Office, Washington, D.C.

USDA (1976b). National food situation. *U.S. Dept. Agr., Econ. Res. Serv.*, NFS–158. 39 pp.

USDA (1977a). Agricultural charts. *Food and Home Notes, No.* 7, Feb. 14.

USDA (1977b). *Firm Enterprise Data System.* USDA, ERS, and Dept. of Agr. Econ., Oklahoma State Univ., Oklahoma.

USDC (1963). *1963 Census of Transportation. Vol.* **III.** *Commodity Transportation Survey.* Part 1 and 2. Commodity groups. U.S. Dept. of Commerce. 471 pp.

USDC (1974). Basic economic indicators: Atlantic and Pacific ground-fish 1932–1972. *U.S. Dept. Commerce, Nat'l. Atmosp. & Ocean. Admin., Nat'l. Marine Fish. Serv., Current Fish. Stat. No.* **6271,** June. U.S. Government Printing Office, Washington, D.C. 106 pp.

USNRB (1935). Soil erosion a critical problem in American agriculture. U.S. Nat'l. Resources Board, Land Planning Committee, Sup. Rep.

U.S. SENATE (1977). *Dietary Goals for the United States.* Select Committee on Nutrition and Human Needs. U.S. Government Printing Office, Washington, D.C. 79 pp.

VAN DEN BOSCH, R. and MESSENGER, P. S. (1973). *Biological Control.* Intext Educational Publishers, New York. 180 pp.

WADLEIGH, C. H. (1968). Wastes in relation to agriculture and forestry. *U.S. Dept. Agr., Misc. Publ.,* **1065.**

WALFORD, C. (1878). The famines of the world: past and present. *J. Roy. Stat. Soc.,* **41,** 433–526.

WALKER, C. and HUNT, R. M. (1973). An analysis of costs for tomato production on the Rockdale soils of south Florida. *Econ. Rep.,* **45.** Food and Resource Economics Dept., Univ. Florida, Gainesville.

WESTOBY, M. and KASE, R. T. (1974). *Catfish Farming and Its Economic Feasibility in New York State.* Unpublished manuscript.

WESTOBY, M., KRUMMEL, J., DRITSCHILO, W. and PIMENTEL, D. (1978). *Direct and Indirect Use of Land, Labor and Fossil Fuels by Some Animal Production Systems.* Manuscript.

WHITE, L. A. (1943). Energy and the evolution of culture. *Am. Anthropol.,* **45,** 335–354.

WHITTAKER, R. H. and LIKENS, G. E. (1975). The biosphere and man. pp. 305–28. In *Primary Productivity of the Biosphere.* H. Lieth and R. H. Whittaker (eds). Springer–Verlag, New York. 339 pp.

WOKES, F. (1968). Proteins. *Pl. Fds. Nutr.,* 1, 23–42.

ZEUNER, F. E. (1963). *A History of Domesticated Animals.* Harper and Row, New York. 560 pp.

Index